OECD Studies on Water

Sustainable Business Models for Water Supply and Sanitation in Small Towns and Rural Settlements in Kazakhstan

This work is published under the responsibility of the Secretary-General of the OECD. The opinions expressed and arguments employed herein do not necessarily reflect the official views of OECD member countries.

This document and any map included herein are without prejudice to the status of or sovereignty over any territory, to the delimitation of international frontiers and boundaries and to the name of any territory, city or area.

Please cite this publication as:
OECD (2016), *Sustainable Business Models for Water Supply and Sanitation in Small Towns and Rural Settlements in Kazakhstan*, OECD Studies on Water, OECD Publishing, Paris.
http://dx.doi.org/10.1787/9789264249400-en

ISBN 978-92-64-24939-4 (print)
ISBN 978-92-64-24940-0 (PDF)

Series: OECD Studies on Water
ISSN 2224-5073 (print)
ISSN 2224-5081 (online)

Photo credits: Cover © Maxim Petrichuk | Dreamstime.com

Corrigenda to OECD publications may be found on line at: *www.oecd.org/about/publishing/corrigenda.htm*.

FOREWORD

This final report was prepared as part of the project on Sustainable Business Models for Water Supply and Sanitation in Small Towns and Rural Areas in Kazakhstan. It was implemented by the OECD EAP Task Force within the framework of the National Policy Dialogue on Water Policy in Kazakhstan in co-operation with the European Union Water Initiative (EUWI) facilitated by the OECD and UNECE. The project was financially supported by the European Union and the governments of Norway and Switzerland.

The key objective was to help Kazakh stakeholders select appropriate business model(s) for the sustainable operation, maintenance and financing of WSS systems in small towns and rural areas. This report presents the results of the analysis, as well as recommended WSS business models for rural areas in Kazakhstan, as part of the expert input into the water policy dialogue. Key findings, conclusions and recommendations of this report were presented at the national WSS seminar in Astana on 4 November 2014. Participants of the seminar recommended presenting the final report to the governmental body responsible for WSS development for consideration in improving state policy for, and elaborating programmes on, WSS development in small towns and rural areas.

The report is divided into several chapters that present the main issues linked to the current complexity and recommendations for further action. The **first part** provides an overview of the WSS sector in Kazakhstan, including current context and legal and institutional framework. The **second part** presents business WSS models prevailing in Kazakhstan, with special emphasis on small towns and rural areas. It outlines several models of WSS services provision and describes the entire range of possible service delivery options. The report ends with a general comparison of prevailing models and lessons learned from their implementation. **A brief overview of business models** in the WSS sector in different EU and EECCA countries is then presented, with an emphasis on lessons learned for Kazakhstan. Based on this analysis and the results of a *Reality Check* (see Annex D), business models for water supply and sanitation in Kazakhstan are then recommended, including the Rayon Vodocanal, community-based management of rural WSS systems, multi-purpose utility and small-scale private operators.

The report concludes with an outline of key steps towards an action plan for recommended sustainable business models in small towns and rural areas for water supply and sanitation in Kazakhstan. A bibliography and several annexes describe in more detail the legal and institutional framework for WSS and the WSS business models identified. They also present several short case studies of WSS sector development and business models applied in selected EU and EECCA countries.

ACKNOWLEDGEMENTS

The project was implemented as part of the National Policy Dialogue (NPD) on water policy in Kazakhstan conducted in co-operation with the European Union Water Initiative (EUWI) in Eastern Europe Caucasus and Central Asia and facilitated by the OECD and the United Nations Economic Commission for Europe (UNECE). The OECD commissioned a group of Polish and Kazakh experts, which included Mr Marian W. Szymanowicz, Mr Rafal Stanek, Mr Igor Petrakov and Mr Zhanat Alyakhassov, for the analytical work. They are authors of this report.

The authors gratefully acknowledge the contribution of participants of the EUWI National Policy Dialogue to the project and to this report, and would like to thank the Committee of Water Resources, the Committee of Architecture, Housing and Utilities, the Centre on Modernising Housing and Communal Services and the Agency of Statistics for their very productive co-operation. The authors are also grateful to the Centre for Water Initiatives for their invaluable support and assistance in implementing the project.

The authors thank Mr Krzysztof Michalak and Mr Xavier Leflaive, former managers of the OECD EAP Task Force Water programme, for their valuable comments that helped improve both the content and structure of the report. In addition, they thank Mr Mark Foss, Ms Meleesa Naughton, external consultant to the OECD and Mr Shukhrat Ziyaviddinov, of the OECD EAP Task Force Secretariat, for editing and formatting the report, respectively. Finally, the authors would like to express their appreciation to the OECD project manager, Mr Alexandre Martoussevitch, for his methodological support, review, valuable comments on, and professional contributions to, the project and to this report.

This publication has been produced with the financial assistance of the European Union and governments of Norway and Switzerland. This support is gratefully acknowledged.

Table of contents

Boxes

Figures

Tables

Abbreviations and Acronyms

AREM	Agency for Regulating Natural Monopolies
BOQ	Bill of Quantity
CEE	Central and Eastern Europe
DFBOT	Design, finance, build, operate, transfer
EAP Task Force	Environmental Action Programme Task Force
EBRD	European Bank for Reconstruction and Development
EC	European Commission
EECCA	Eastern Europe, Caucasus and Central Asia
EUR	Euro (currency unit of the European monetary union)
EU	European Union
EUWI	European Union Water Initiative
IFI	international financing institution
IMC	inter-municipal co-operation
KZT	tenge (currency of Kazakhstan)
lcd	litres per capita per day
LPA	local public administration
MDG	Millennium Development Goals
MoENV	Ministry of Environment
MRD	Ministry of Regional Development
NPD	National Policy Dialogue
OECD	Organisation for Economic Co-operation and Development
O&M	operation and maintenance
PE	person equivalent
PPP	public-private partnership

PPP	purchasing power parity
RK	the Republic of Kazakhstan
UNECE	United Nations Economic Commission for Europe
WRM	water resources management
WS	water supply
WSS	water supply & sanitation
WWT	wastewater treatment
WWTP	wastewater treatment plant

General Notes:

The model of water supply and sanitation (WSS) service delivery by a ***community-based organisation*** *refers to the delivery of services by a voluntary* ***association or co-operative*** *of drinking water users created by the local population and/or other stakeholders.*

The term ***Vodocanal*** *refers to water utility functioning in the form of a publicly-owned enterprise.*

Local governments *refer to local public authorities and local self-governance bodies.*

The term ***grouped water mains*** *refers to water pipes that carry water across long distances to settlements that have no water sources of their own and have to rely on alternative and distant water sources. They are typically inter-municipal or inter-rayonal, or even inter-regional systems.*

Exchange rates *as of mid-Dec., 2014: USD 1 = KZT 182; EUR 1 = KZT 226*

Executive Summary

Kazakhstan has made significant efforts to improve the water supply and sanitation sector, but much remains to be done

Over the last 15 years, the government of the Republic of Kazakhstan has made significant efforts to improve water supply and sanitation (WSS) services. It has set ambitious targets, established a sound water tariff policy and invested significant public funds in the rehabilitation and development of relevant infrastructure. The investments were initially undertaken within the framework of the government's Drinking Water Programme (2001-10). Further actions followed under the *Ak Bulak* programme, which established ambitious objectives to reduce persistent disparities between urban and rural areas for WSS coverage. Specifically, it sought to provide 80% of the rural population and 100% of small town residents with centralised water supply services by 2020.

The Ak Bulak programme provided a needed push for developing new rural water supply systems. To that end, it created new operators, replicating the municipal WSS utility model. However, many did not survive the first years of operation, leaving systems non-operational and undermining the value of public investments. That was one key reason why the significant efforts to build and rehabilitate WSS infrastructure in small towns and rural areas have not fully reached their potential.

Given this recent experience, there is an urgent need to review the business models of WSS operations to ensure their long-term sustainability, efficiency and effectiveness. Moreover, this must take place before massive new investments are made. In doing so, more attention is needed to improve access to sanitation systems in rural areas to match the progress in providing access to water.

The sustainability of WSS business models remains a key issue, as prevailing management models have limitations and often face problems

There are no available official data on the percentage of rural population served by different business models. Most experts suggest that WSS services provided by large farms and agriculture enterprises is one of the most prevalent in rural areas. Together with small private operators, this model delivers WSS services to about two-thirds of the rural population, especially in the eastern and northern regions. Small town water utilities, including a multi-services utility and rayon water utility, service most of the remaining third. Community-based organisations service only a small share of the rural population.

The review of existing business models in small towns and rural areas in Kazakhstan shows their development has been largely ad hoc rather than planned. In most cases, the currently applied models are not suited to the local geographic, hydrological, technical, financial and social conditions.

Although the WSS services provided by agriculture farms are prevalent, they have no expertise in providing services other than for their own needs; this often results in inadequate service delivery. Inadequate operation and maintenance (O&M) lead to frequent technical breakdowns and irregular water delivery. Most operate without legally valid licences and lack the appropriate technical documentation for O&M. In areas where decentralised small town water utilities provide services, the analysis shows failures to create economies of scale due to the restricted size of the service area. The Rayon Vodocanal model, recommended under the Ak Bulak programme, is implemented without adequate institutional planning and financial analysis, thereby threatening its sustainability. In all models, the affordability of services for residents is usually not analysed, thereby failing to implement effective social policies for providing the poor with basic services.

Overall, experience suggests that a systematic approach to the institutional development of WSS service operators is crucial. The lack of sustainable WSS business models in rural areas and small towns threatens the sustainability of existing systems. In so doing, it undermines the effectiveness of the government's interventions to bridge the gap in access between urban and rural areas, including small towns and villages. The identification and implementation of sustainable WSS business models for WSS in rural areas and small towns needs to be at the top of the WSS development policy agenda in Kazakhstan.

Lessons learned from international experience in WSS management: Consolidation vs. Delegation of WSS services delivery

Although there is no universal "first best" model for the management of WSS services, especially in small towns and rural areas, international experience provides important lessons for developing Kazakhstan's WSS sector.

This report reviews WSS management models in selected countries of the European Union (EU) and Eastern Europe, Caucasus and Central Asia (EECCA). It analyses two main factors for determining appropriate WSS business models: the level of sector **consolidation** and the degree of **delegation** of service delivery. Regarding the applicability of the reviewed WSS business models to the small towns and rural settlements of Kazakhstan, the following observations are highlighted:

- Considering the low population density, the decentralised model is not recommended for small towns and most rural areas in Kazakhstan. It does not create the required economies of scale or address the lack of capacity of small-scale water and wastewater operators. The voluntary regionalisation of WSS services would be time-consuming and could be implemented only with the appropriate fiscal and economic incentives. Thus, the most appropriate option is mandatory regionalisation of WSS services. However, international experience shows it cannot be implemented without both state support and certain kinds of complementary of business models.
- International experience shows that in case of direct provision by local authorities WSS service provision is often politicized. Many countries address this problem by creating limited liability or joint stock companies. Community-based organisations and small private operators could be considered as complementary business models. As for private sector participation, international review shows it requires a strong enabling environment (removing any administrative obstacles); however, public authorities in Kazakhstan have had so far limited experience in applying this model.
- Utilities that provide several services, such as WSS, district heating and municipal waste management in many countries, could be another alternative solution for Kazakhstan to achieve economies of scope. However, this model could only be

applied in towns or rayons where other municipal services (e.g. district heating) are already in place. It would also require a solid accounting system to correctly apportion overhead costs between the services provided. The optimal approach would be to apply this model as a second step, after the regionalisation process.

- Regardless of delegation level of WSS services, the selected WSS business model must be financially sustainable (i.e. revenue from user charges should cover the costs of service provision, including O&M; possibly the renewal of infrastructure; and, ideally, extension).

Two key criteria for selecting sustainable business models: Population density and affordability

Kazakhstan has a **very low population density** of 6.3 persons per square kilometre (km^2) on average, and as low as 2.8 persons per km^2 in rural areas. This means that in many rural areas, population density and economic activity are not sufficient to develop economically justified and affordable centralised WSS systems. As a result, in a large part of Kazakhstan's territory (the least populated area), WSS services are, and will continue to be, based on individual self-supply solutions. At best, small villages and communities will manage their own WSS systems.

With income for rural households lower than in urban areas, many more people live in poverty in rural than in urban areas. Consequently, the **affordability of WSS services** is one of the key factors determining the sustainability of WSS business models for rural areas. **A local affordability analysis and willingness to pay study should therefore be conducted** as part of the economic analysis of the selected WSS model to ensure its financial sustainability. Small towns and rural areas should do a micro- affordability analysis, while a macro-affordability analysis is more suitable for medium-sized and large cities.

Recommendations for Kazakhstan

Taking into account lessons learned from international experience and WSS sector development in Kazakhstan, the recommended solution is the consolidation and regionalisation of water utilities at the rayon level, through the application of the **Rayon Vodocanal model.** This model will help create a minimal size of the served population to benefit from economies of scale. It will also address the existing constraints related to local technical and management capacity, which is limited or absent in many rural settlements. This model will also allow a uniform tariff throughout the service area, helping small and poor villages to address affordability constraints.

The Rayon Vodocanal, acting on behalf of Rayon Administration, should also be responsible for: (a) providing back-stopping assistance to the community-based and other small-scale operators of WSS systems in the rayon (e.g. leak detection, major repairs); and (b) monitoring the provision of WSS services in the entire territory of the rayon.

Community-based management of WSS services should complement the Rayon Vodocanal model, which uses regionalisation to address the inefficient (too small) service zone size. Community-based management addresses the challenge of small distant rural WSS centralised systems that will not be served by the Rayon Vodocanal for economic reasons.

There are examples of successes and failures in community-based management of WSS services in Kazakhstan. International experience suggests, however, that this model works, provided it benefits from continuous external technical assistance. The investment in technical assistance at the local level should be viewed as a way to ensure long-term sustainability of community management of WSS services.

Many countries facing challenges similar to Kazakhstan have also successfully applied the model of **private operators** of small-scale WSS systems in rural areas. For example, some have extended the provision of services of private companies already on the WSS market. This model may also be a suitable option for Kazakhstan, but the legal, institutional and regulatory framework for small-scale public-private partnership (PPP) arrangements would need to be reviewed. Taking into account Kazakhstan's low population density, it would also require grouping villages, where feasible, to create more favourable conditions for private operators.

Improving the legal framework for implementing the recommended WSS business models

The *Reality Check* demonstrated the current legal framework already allows for the development of the Rayon Vodocanal and the community-managed WSS models. However, it also showed the existing legal framework should be reviewed and improved for the effective application of the recommended WSS business models. In particular, Rayon local authorities should be empowered to develop the Rayon Vodocanal model, while village authorities in the WSS sector should be supported to help local communities develop community-based management of WSS services. In addition, the current PPP legal framework should be reviewed to allow small-scale arrangements at village, small town and rayon levels. Currently, there is a window of opportunity to consider elaborating a dedicated law on WSS services. Such a **sectoral WSS law** would create a solid legal base for the development of WSS services in the entire country, and remains one of the most important objectives of the Ak Bulak programme.

The **Rayon WSS Development Plan, or WSS Master Plan**, is recommended as a useful tool for decision making. In addition to engineering designs for WSS infrastructure, the plan should analyse a variety of WSS business models. Among models that best suit local hydrological, engineering, financial, and social conditions, it should select ones that are feasible and affordable. It must outline the proposed WSS business models at the local level and their respective service areas in the mid- and long-term. The plan should also indicate which areas will have to rely on self-supply of WSS services; those which are or will be under community management of WSS services; and those where WSS services are or will be delivered by other institutional models, such as the rayon water utility.

The local population living in territories adjacent to the WSS service area should have the right to participate in the decision-making process. This will allow them to determine whether they would rather receive WSS services from a rayon WSS operator or from their own community management organisation (co-operative or association).

To cover WSS development across a larger area, the rayon WSS Development Plans may need to be co-ordinated with, or approved by, the respective oblast public authorities. Central and oblast governments should provide financial and technical assistance to rural rayons in developing and implementing WSS Development Plans. This includes adopting and disseminating methodological and guidance documents, as well as training officers of rayon administrations responsible for WSS.

The absence of updated data on WSS institutional development limits WSS development policies and programmes in many countries, including Kazakhstan. The monitoring and evaluation system proposed in this report would help assess progress in the WSS sector and serve as a basis for any necessary corrective measures. This is especially important as developing Rayon Vodocanals and community management of WSS services will take time, and will need to be monitored closely. Monitoring of WSS sector development at the rayon level should be aggregated at the oblast and national levels.

Chapter 1.

General Information on Water Supply and Sanitation in Kazakhstan

This section presents background information on the water supply and sanitation (WSS) sector in Kazakhstan. It highlights such key factors influencing selection of appropriate business model as low density of population, substantial number of remote villages and uneven distribution of fresh water resources suitable for drinking water supply across the territory of the country.

Administrative organisation and rural development programmes

Kazakhstan has a territory of 2.7 million square kilometres (km^2) and a population of approximately 17.1 million people, resulting in a population density of 6.3 people per km^2. Kazakhstan has one of the lowest population densities in the world, close to that of the Russian Federation (8.3 people per km^2). In Kazakhstan, 9 436 900 people reside in urban areas (55%), and 7 661 650 in rural areas (44%). If one takes into account the population of rural areas only, population density is much lower, with an average 2.8 persons per km^2. Currently, the territory of Kazakhstan is divided into 14 oblasts and 2 cities of republican subordination (Astana and Almaty), which have a status of oblast administration.[1] The country is further divided into 175 rayons and 7 002 rural communities.[2] At the lowest administrative level, there are 87 cities[3], 33 towns, and 6 869 villages. The population density varies from as low as 2.7 people per km^2 in Aktyubinsk Oblast to 23.2 people per km^2 in South Kazakhstan Oblast. Tables 1.1-1.3 below present some key information and figures on the administrative and territorial organisation of Kazakhstan, the number of residents and population density, as well as rural communities and villages by oblast.

Table 1.1. Territory and population of oblasts in 2013

No	Oblast or city of republican subordination	Oblast centre	Territory km²	Population no. of people	Density no. of people/km²
1	Akmola Oblast	Kokchetau	146 219	735 232	5.03
2	Aktyubinsk Oblast	Aktobe	300 629	805 117	2.68
3	Almaty Oblast	Taldykorgan	223 911	1 977 324	8.83
4	Atyrau Oblast	Atyrau	118 631	564 936	4.76
5	East Kazakhstan Oblast	Ust-Kamenogorsk	283 226	1 394 382	4.92
6	Zhambyl Oblast	Taraz	144 264	1 081 907	7.50
7	West Kazakhstan Oblast	Uralsk	151 339	622 333	4.11
8	Karaganda Oblast	Karaganda	427 982	1 367 512	3.20
9	Kostanay Oblast	Kostanay	196 001	880 775	4.49
10	Kyzylorda Oblast	Kyzylorda	226 074	776 092	3.43
11	Mangistau Oblast	Aktau	165 642	582 361	3.52
12	Pavlodar Oblast	Pavlodar	124 755	752 057	6.03
13	North Kazakhstan Oblast	Petropavlovsk	97 993	526 748	5.89
14	South Kazakhstan Oblast	Shymkent	117 249	2 721 676	23.21
15	Astana – city of Republican subordination	n/a	710	804 474	1 133.06
16	Almaty – city of Republican subordination	n/a	451	1 494 590	3 313.95

Source: The Agency of Statistics, www.stat.gov.kz.

Table 1.2. Territory and population of rayons, by oblast, in 2013

No	Oblast	Number of rayons	Average territory of rayon, km2	Average population of rayon; No. of residents
1	Akmola Oblast	17	8 601	43 249
2	Aktyubinsk Oblast	12	25 052	67 093
3	Almaty Oblast	16	13 994	123 583
4	Atyrau Oblast	7	16 947	80 705
5	East Kazakhstan Oblast	15	18 882	92 959
6	Zhambyl Oblast	10	14 426	108 191
7	West Kazakhstan Oblast	12	12 612	51 861
8	Karaganda Oblast	9	47 554	151 946
9	Kostanay Oblast	16	12 250	55 048
10	Kyzylorda Oblast	7	32 288	105 303
11	Mangistau Oblast	4	41 411	145 590
12	Pavlodar Oblast	10	12 476	75 206
13	North Kazakhstan Oblast	13	7 538	40 519
14	South Kazakhstan Oblast	12	9 771	226 806

Source: The Agency of Statistics, www.stat.gov.kz.

Table 1.3. Rural communities and villages, by oblast, in 2013

No	Oblast	Number of rural communities	Number of villages	Average number of villages in a rural community
1	Akmola Oblast	236	712	3.02
2	Aktyubinsk Oblast	141	441	3.13
3	Almaty Oblast	251	759	3.02
4	Atyrau Oblast	71	189	2.66
5	East Kazakhstan Oblast	252	857	3.40
6	Zhambyl Oblast	153	367	2.40
7	West Kazakhstan Oblast	155	475	3.06
8	Karaganda Oblast	192	498	2.59
9	Kostanay Oblast	256	769	3.00
10	Kyzylorda Oblast	143	269	1.88
11	Mangistau Oblast	43	49	1.14
12	Pavlodar Oblast	169	505	2.99
13	North Kazakhstan Oblast	204	932	4.57
14	South Kazakhstan Oblast	187	689	3.68

Source: The Agency of Statistics, www.stat.gov.kz.

Water resources

According to the Committee of Water Resources of the Republic of Kazakhstan, around 37 000 m^3 of fresh water is available per km^2; this amounts to 6 000 m^3 of renewable freshwater per capita per year. In terms of renewable freshwater per capita, Kazakhstan is placed in the medium of OECD member countries, close to Greece (6 490 m^3), Switzerland (6 585 m^3) and Portugal (6 999 m^3).[4] There are eight river basins in Kazakhstan, out of which the largest are the Yertis, Balkhash-Alakol, Aral-Syr Darya and Caspian Sea; jointly, they account for over 70% of surface fresh water resources available (Table 1.4).

Renewable surface fresh water resources in Kazakhstan amount to 100.5 km^3 during an average year, of which only 56.5 km^3 is generated on the territory of the republic. The remaining 44.0 km^3 come from neighbouring countries: from China (18.9 km^3), followed by Uzbekistan (14.6 km^3), Kyrgyzstan (3.0 km^3) and the Russian Federation (7.5 km^3). The average water abstraction as a percentage of renewable fresh water resources in OECD member countries is about 10%[5], while in Kazakhstan it reaches 18.6%.[6]

Table 1.4. Fresh water resources in the Republic of Kazakhstan, in 2012

No.	Water basin	Average long-term flow (mln m³)			Groundwater (mln m³)	
		Flow outside of the Republic of Kazakhstan	Flow within the Republic of Kazakhstan	Total	Projected resources	Known and validated reserves
1	Aral-Syr Darya	14 630	3 360	17 990	9 290.2	1 134.53
2	Balkhash-Alakol	12 247	15 434	27 681	20 012.1	7 257.96
3	Yertis	7 780	25 920	33 700	9 563.7	2 867.76
4	Yesil	-	2 588	2 588	2 313.5	164.39
5	Zhayik Caspian	7 108	4 130	11 238	7 373.3	966.19
6	Nura-Sarysu	-	1 365.7	1 365.7	3 314.4	823.84
7	Tobyl-Torgay	292	1 577.6	1 869.6	3 620.5	479.13
8	Shu-Talas	2 604	1 640	4 244	8 791	1 748.05
Total		44 661	56 015	100 676	64 278.5	15 441.85

Source: Committee of Water Resources of the Ministry of Agriculture of the Republic of Kazakhstan, www.eco.gov.kz/new2012/ministry/komitet/kvr/.

In 2010, freshwater use amounted to 20 856 million m3, 751 million m3 of which was used for domestic water supply (Figure 1.1):

Figure 1.1. Use of water by communal sector, industry, agriculture and other sectors, in 2010

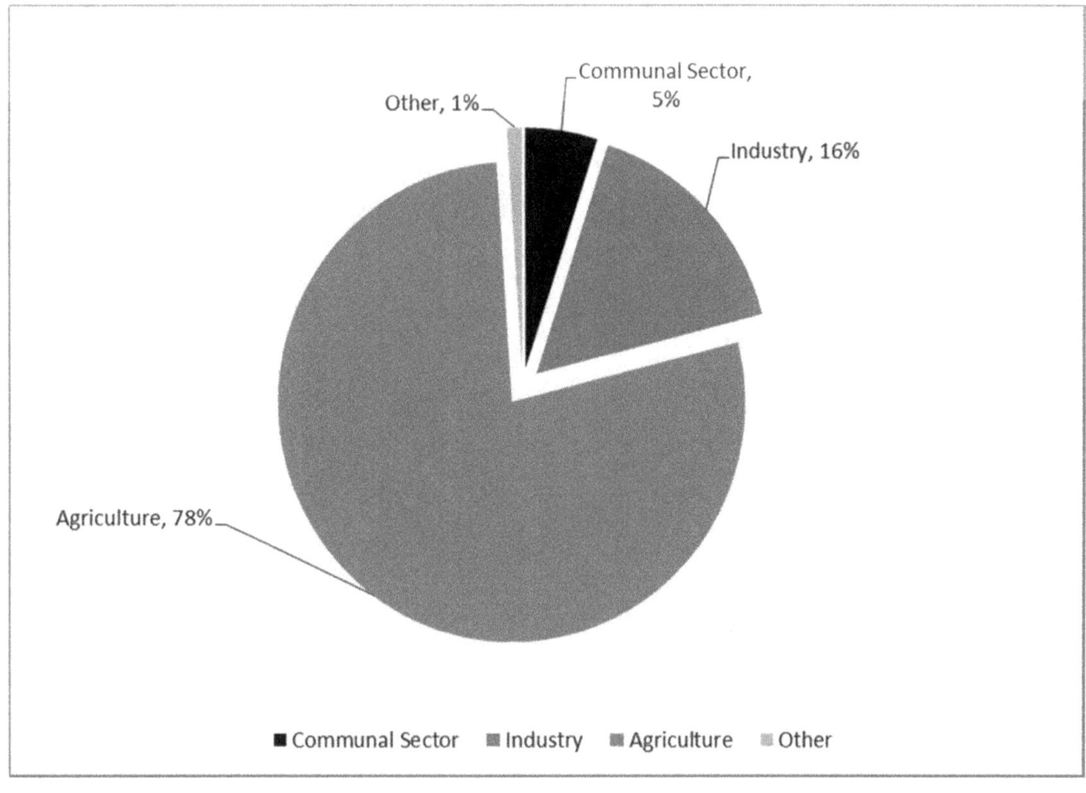

Source: Committee of Water Resources of the Ministry of Agriculture of the Republic of Kazakhstan.

Groundwater is distributed unevenly throughout the territory of Kazakhstan. Groundwater resources in southern and eastern Kazakhstan exceed water demand manifold, while the northern, western and central regions face a severe shortage of groundwater. Out of 494 aquifers suitable for domestic water supply purposes, 343 were put into commercial exploitation. This resulted in an average total groundwater abstraction of 2 901 000 m^3/day in Kazakhstan for domestic water supply purposes, i.e. 17% of groundwater reserves available for exploitation.

Available groundwater resources have been used at an extremely slow pace, or their use has been suspended almost completely in a number of regions in recent years. Data presented in Figure 1.2 suggest that, in the northern and western oblasts, abstraction from surface water is higher than in the south, which relies on groundwater for domestic and industrial water supply. Box 1.1 highlights challenges related to water stress and pollution while Box 1.2 discusses impact of climate change.

Figure 1.2. Water abstraction for domestic and industrial water supply in Kazakhstan in 2011

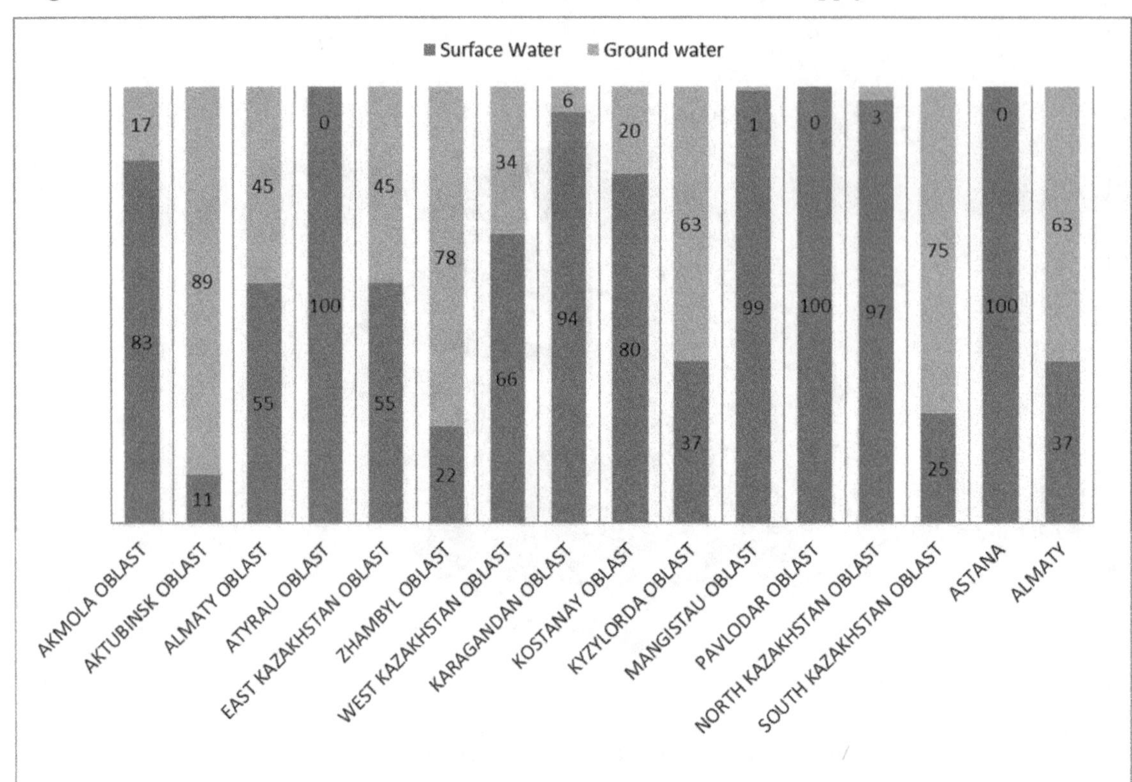

Source: Committee of Water Resources of the Ministry of Agriculture of the Republic of Kazakhstan, www.eco.gov.kz/new2012/ministry/komitet/kvr/

Box 1.1. **Two key challenges: Water stress and pollution of fresh water resources**

Water stress: In 2012, the Nura-Sarysu River Basin experienced a shortage of available, sustainable and reliable water resources of 0.1 km3 a year. In practice, this means insufficient environmental flows (the flow of water for environmental purposes that is essential for maintaining river and lake ecosystems). By 2020, due to less trans-boundary flow caused by the reduction of available resources, and due to more water consumption upstream, six out of the eight river basins of Kazakhstan will experience freshwater shortages. The deficit will keep increasing up to the 2040 horizon and could amount to 12.2 km3 a year (50% of projected net consumption). If upstream neighbouring states increase freshwater abstraction, a further 7.5 km3 of freshwater could become unavailable. The situation will be particularly critical in the Aral-Syr Darya and Zhayik Caspian Basins (with freshwater shortages in absolute terms of 4.1 km3 and 2.9 km3 per year respectively) and in the Nura-Sarysu and Tobyl-Torgay Basins, where the shortage will account for over 50% of projected water use. Due to the rapidly growing demand for water and the decline in sustainable water reserves, the water shortage is expected to reach 14 bln m3 by 2030 and 20 bln m3 by 2050 (i.e. 70% of projected demand) unless drastic action is taken. Economic losses related to water risks are estimated to amount to USD 6-7 bln a year by 2030, while the cost of transition to a water resource efficient economy remains smaller (USD 0.5-1 bln a year).

Water pollution. The quality of water resources is degraded by activities from the mining, metallurgical and chemical sectors, as well as municipal utility services, all of which pose a serious threat to the environment. Yertis, Nura, Syr Darya, and Ili rivers, as well as Lake Balkhash, are the most polluted water bodies. Groundwater, which is the main source of drinking water supply for the population, is also exposed to pollution. Water is polluted mostly because many regions, cities and industries fail to ensure wastewater treatment; the condition of water sources does not comply with standards; and groundwater gets dangerously polluted by numerous sewage ponds or other utility, industrial or agricultural facilities.

Source: Kazhydromet.

Box 1.2. **Expected impacts of climate change**

There is a consensus in academia that climate change will make Kazakhstan “drier” on average and will lead to a decrease of surface water levels. Climate change will result in increasingly uneven distribution of precipitation, frequent floods and snowstorms, larger scale of droughts, shortage of water resources available, especially in the spring and the summer, seasons. This will lead to a decline in agricultural yields as plants are expected to grow much slower, if at all, in extreme temperatures.

Winter precipitation is projected to increase on average by 8% in 2030, by 13% in 2050 and by 24% in 2086. Summer precipitation will decrease by 5% in 2030, remain constant between 2030-50 and decrease by 11% in 2085. According to experts from RGP Kazhydromet, the weather in Kazakhstan has become quite extreme: for instance, a recent heat wave, which spread over many regions and caused major harm to agriculture, was followed by heavy rains, strong winds and thunderstorms, with daily precipitation exceeding the monthly norm in some regions. Monthly average temperature anomalies amounted to 3-5 °C. The likelihood of mudslides and flooding has increased. The scale of emergency situations in the mountain water reservoirs in Almaty, Kyzylorda and East Kazakhstan Oblasts is a direct consequence of climate change.

Source: Kazhydromet.

Water supply and sanitation coverage and quality of services

As of 2012, according to the Agency of the Republic of Kazakhstan for Architecture, Housing and Utilities, 84% of the urban population had access to centralised water supply, while 75% had access to centralised sanitation systems. The information on WSS coverage and quality of services in rural areas is fragmented and not easily accessible. It is estimated that only 45% of the rural population has access to a centralised drinking water supply, and only 9% to centralised wastewater systems. In addition, 153 villages (2.2% of the total number) use water transported by water tanks as the source of drinking water supply.

The agency further reports that most water supply networks are in unsatisfactory condition. Only 36% are working, and about 64% require rehabilitation or complete replacement: most water supply networks were developed 25-40 years ago and are beyond their design lifetime. The total length of sanitation networks in the cities is 12 890 km (half of the length of the drinking water network), which shows the disparity in the development of water supply networks and sewerage systems.

From 2002-10, the number of non-operational water supply systems (those left without an operator), or totally obsolete declined from 299 to 209. During the same period, the number of systems non-compliant with sanitary and epidemiological requirements decreased from 336 to 133.

In 2012, an average of 76.4 litres of water per capita and per day (lcd) was supplied to residents.[7] Some areas received a higher amount of water than the national average, including Pavlodar Oblast (1.7 times higher than the national average), Atyrau Oblast (1.5 times higher), Karaganda Oblast (1.6 times higher), and the cities of Almaty (1.9 times higher) and Astana (1.5 times higher). On the other hand, the lowest amounts of water consumed were in Almaty Oblast and Kyzylorda Oblast (1.8 times lower than the national average), Akmola Oblast (1.1 times lower), Zhambyl Oblast (1.7 times lower), West Kazakhstan Oblast (1.4 lower) and South Kazakhstan Oblast (1.4 times lower).

Water supply to the network amounted to 2.1 billion m^3, more than a quarter of which was treated at water treatment plants. Physical and commercial water losses represented on average 15-20%, with the losses in Almaty reaching 40%.[8]

According to the National Statistics Agency, 609 wastewater treatment plants and 387 stand-alone sanitation networks were operational throughout the republic in 2012. Wastewater treatment plants have a total installed capacity of 4 137 000 m^3 per day and treated 678.9 mln m^3 of wastewater per year, i.e. 88.4% of total wastewater flow. In addition, 544.6 mln m^3 of wastewater, or 80.2% of total wastewater flow, received a complete biological treatment.

While water supply systems have been developing at a rapid pace, the condition of the sanitation network is poor in small towns and rural settlements.

Water tariffs and affordability

The government's recent priorities include an effective tariff policy based on balancing the interests of consumers with those of the WSS sector, as well as improving the tariff calculation system for natural monopolies in regulated markets, like WSS.[9] The objective is to attract investment to the WSS sector in order to modernise and upgrade infrastructure, improve the quality of services and increase competitiveness. As a consequence of implementing this policy, water tariffs were adjusted recently to reflect actual costs in the WSS sector. According to the Agency of Statistics of the Republic of Kazakhstan, on average in 2013, drinking water tariffs in the country increased by 46.2%, while tariffs for sewerage services by 43.6%; annual inflation was approximately 6.0%. See Table 1.5 for water tariffs in selected cities of the Republic of Kazakhstan in 2013.

Table 1.5.Water tariffs in selected cities of the Republic of Kazakhstan

Name of water utility	User group	Old tariff rate (KZT/m³)	New tariff rate (KZT/m³)	Tariff increase	
				in KZT/m3	in %
Effective 01 January 2013					
JSC Ak Bulak, Aktobe (pop. 427 719)	With IMs*	30.34	55.4	25	83
	Without IMs	30.34	72.0	42	137
GKP Taraz Su, Taraz (pop. 351 476)	With IMs	19.36	22.8	3	18
	Without IMs	28.94	105.9	77	266
Effective 1 February 2013					
GKP Zhetysu Su Arnasy, Taldykorgan (pop. 159 037)		35.97	51.74	16	44
GKP Bastau, Almaty	With IMs	23.50	28.08	4	19
	Without IMs	23.50	62.00	39	164
TOO Batys Su Arnasy, Uralsk	With IMs	22.44	38.16	16	70
	Without IM	22.44	57.15	35	155
Effective 1 April 2013					
GKP Kostanay Su, Kostanay (pop. 221 970)	With IMs	47.67	60.14	12	26
	Without IMs	47.67	66.83	19	40
GKP Atyrau Su Arnasy, Atyrau (pop. 281 479)	With IMs	28.00	32.14	4	15
	Without IMs	32.48	60.14	28	85
TOO Pavlodar Vodocanal, Pavlodar (pop. 350 998)	With IMs	21.60	21.60	0	0
	Without IMs	24.62	31.83	7	29

Note: * - **IM** stands for "individual meter"

Source: AREM KZ: www.arem.kz.

One objective of the new water tariffs policy is to persuade consumers to reduce water consumption. This could be achieved through installation of individual water meters and the introduction of differentiated water tariffs. Table 1.5 shows that water tariff rates for customers without individual water meters are higher than for customers with individual water meters. As of 1 July 2010, according to the Agency on Regulation of Natural Monopolies of the Republic of Kazakhstan, 76% of households had individual water meters (**IMs**); in rural areas, the figure was around 40%.

In 2013, according to the same agency, sewerage tariff rates increased in Atyrau, Kostanay and Pavlodar Oblasts. In Atyrau Oblast, sewerage tariff rates increased by 12.5%

for an average rate of KZT 27 per m^3 of wastewater. In Kostanay Oblast, sewerage tariff rates increased by 46% for an average rate of KZT 48.8 per m^3 of wastewater. In Pavlodar Oblast, rates increased by 15% for an average rate of KZT 15.24 per m^3 of wastewater. Lower tariff rates for sewerage services compared to drinking water underscores that sewerage infrastructure, including wastewater treatment plants, is not yet fully developed. Normally, in cases of developed sewerage infrastructure and advanced wastewater treatment technology, sewerage tariffs are higher than drinking water tariffs, reflecting higher capital and O&M costs.

Table 1.6 shows selected macroeconomic indicators in the Republic of Kazakhstan for the period of 2001-10.

Table 1.6.Selected macroeconomic indicators of the Republic of Kazakhstan in 2001-10

Indicator	2001	2002	2003	2004	2005	2006	2007	2008	2009	2010
Nominal cash income of the population, monthly average per capita, KZT (estimated)	7 670	8 958	10 533	12 817	15 787	19 152	25 226	32 984	34 282	40 473
Monthly average nominal wage, KZT	17 303	20 323	23 128	28 329	34 060	40 790	52 479	60 8 05	67 333	77 6 11
Monthly average pension (at year-end)[3], KZT	4 947	5 818	8 198	8 628	9 061	9 898	10 654	13 418	17 090	21 238
Subsistence minimum[4] (average per capita), KZT	5 655	6 003	6 457	6 785	7 618	8 410	9 653	12 364	12 660	13 487

Source: The Agency of Statistics, www.stat.gov.kz.

The census of 2009 showed a 13.8% increase in the number of households in Kazakhstan, compared to 1999. While the number of urban and rural households increased by 13.4% and 30.3% respectively. The average household size decreased in both urban and rural areas: according to the 2009 census, the average household size was 3.5 persons. Households consisting of two people accounted for 30.1% of total; of three people, 26.7%; of four people, 22.2%; of five people, 11.7%; of six people 5.6%; and of seven people and more, 2.1%.

A critical factor for the sustainability of WSS service delivery is the balance between **full cost recovery** from water tariffs and its **affordability** for the population. Rapid GDP and household income growth over 2001-10, has soften the affordability problem (see Box 1.3).

Box 1.3. Affordability: Macro data

According to the Agency of Statistics, from 2001-10, the nominal gross domestic product (GDP) of the Republic of Kazakhstan nearly tripled, reaching USD 16 203/2 948 946 KZT per capita. At the same time, the average nominal income per capita per month increased by 5.3 times, amounting to KZT 40 473. From 2001, the percentage of the population with income below the poverty line was reduced by 7.2 times; in 2010, it remained at 6.5%, thereby maintaining the trend in reduced extreme poverty both for urban and rural areas. According to household surveys, the percentage of the population with incomes below the subsistence minimum in Kazakhstan in Q1 of 2013 was 3.1% (519 200 people), which is 0.8 percentage points lower than for Q1 of the previous year. In Q2 of 2013, 3.2% of the population of Kazakhstan (i.e. 541 700 people) had incomes below the minimum for subsistence, which is 0.9 percentage points in Q2 of the previous year. In rural areas, the percentage of people with incomes below the subsistence level was higher than in urban areas and amounted to 5.0% (i.e. 382 400 people) in Q1 of 2013, and 5.5% (421 800 people) in Q2 of 2013.

Source: The Agency of Statistics.

Taking into account the statistical information presented above, although water tariffs were significantly increased recently, they are still within the range of affordability in urban areas. In rural areas water tariffs are higher, while the financial situation of households is worse than in urban areas; hence, affordability constraints are greater.

The OECD conducted one of the most extensive studies on water affordability worldwide (OECD, 2003). The study distinguishes between macro-affordability (average national water expenditure divided by average household income) and micro-affordability (which includes estimates differentiated by income group, family type and geographic region). It confirms the importance of analysing different income groups (Fankhauser and Tepic, 2005). In Kazakhstan, and in EECCA in general, as a household grows its per capita income declines, and the share of water charges in household expenditures grows.

The macro-affordability analysis in Kazakhstan shows that current water tariffs, even after the recent tariff increases, are still within the affordability criteria (i.e. expenses for WSS are less than 4% of household disposable income); however, the situation in small towns and rural areas is most likely different because i) average household disposable income is much lower than in medium-sized and large cities; ii) household size is much larger (six to eight people on average); and iii) water tariffs are higher. Although households in rural areas consume less water (in lcd) than in urban areas, this does not compensate for the differences in the level of water tariffs and household incomes.

As a result, people in some rural areas refuse to use the centralised water supply because they cannot afford it. In the opinion of experts, affordability analyses should be part of feasibility studies undertaken locally, at the level of the rayon. In the example of micro-affordability analysis in Box 1.4 and Table 1.7, high water tariffs may be well above the affordability threshold for low-income households in rural areas.

Box 1.4. Example of affordability analysis

- Family size: option minimum (FS-Min) - six people, and option maximum (FS-Max) - eight people.
- Household income: option minimum (HI-Min) – KZT 63 668.5/month, option average (HI-Aver) – KZT 135 329.13/month.
- Water tariff: option minimum (WT-Min) – KZT 40/1m3, option maximum (WT-Max) – KZT 150 /1m3.
- Water consumption: option minimum (WC-Min) – 50 lcd, option maximum (WC-Max) – 150 lcd.

Table 1.7 provides a calculation of affordability for the above scenarios.

Table 1.7. Affordability of water tariffs based on different scenarios

Scenario	Average bill [KZT/month]	WSS expenses as percentage of household income
FS-Min, HI-Min, WT-Min, WC-Min	403.2	0.6
FS-Min, HI-Min, WT-Min, WC-Max	1 209.6	1.9
FS-Min, HI-Min, WT-Max, WC-Min	1512.0	2.4
FS-Min, HI-Min, WT-Max, WC-Max	4 536.0	7.1
FS-Max, HI-Min, WT-Max, WC-Max	6 048.0	9.5
FS-Min, HI-Aver, WT-Min, WC-Min	403.2	0.3
FS-Min, HI-Aver, WT-Min, WC-Max	1 209.6	0.9
FS-Min, HI-Min, WT-Max, WC-Min	1 512.0	1.1
FS-Min, HI-Aver, WT-Max, WC-Max	4 536.0	3.4
FS-Max, HI-Aver, WT-Max, WC-Max	6 048.0	4.5

Source: Authors' own calculations.

For low-income families, only the minimum tariff of KZT 40/m^3 is affordable for the highest volume of water consumption (which is the average water consumption in Kazakhstan) or a higher tariff with the minimum consumption of 50 lcd. Higher rates of water consumption exceed the level of affordability of water (lines **in bold**). This example of affordability calculation illustrates that, in the case of small towns and rural areas, the affordability analysis should be done locally to analyse specific local conditions.

Programmes for the development of the water supply and sanitation sector

In 2002, recognising WSS development as a priority, the government of the Republic of Kazakhstan adopted a Drinking Water Programme for the period of 2002-10 (Decree No. 93 of 23 January 2002). The main objective was to increase access to adequate quality/safe drinking water by extending the number of connections to centralised water supply systems. The Ministry of Agriculture co-ordinated the programme, which was implemented in two phases (2002-05 and 2006-10). Financing (around KZT 194.9 bn, i.e. 65% of planned funds) was allocated from the state budget, with the remainder coming from local budgets and the private sector. As a result, 13 288 km of water lines were reconstructed and repaired, and water supply systems were improved in 3 449 rural settlements, including 32 small towns. Altogether, about 50 000 people received access to quality drinking water, including 35 000 people in rural areas (0.2% of the total population of Kazakhstan). However, despite this progress, the programme did not reach all planned indicators, which led to the creation of another WSS programme (Box 1.5).

Box 1.5. The Ak Bulak programme

On 24 May 2011, the government of the Republic of Kazakhstan adopted the Ak Bulak Programme for 2011-20 to provide the population with quality drinking water and sanitation services. By 2020, 100% of the urban population and 80% of the rural population are expected to have access to centralised drinking water. At the same time, 100% of the urban population and 20% of the rural population will have access to sewerage systems. The programme objectives are the following:

- Introduce a systematic approach for the construction and/or rehabilitation of water and sanitation infrastructure.
- Construct and rehabilitate centralised water supply and sanitation systems in urban areas.
- Construct and rehabilitate centralised water supply and local sanitation systems (septic tanks) in rural areas.
- Improve the legal regulatory framework in the field of water supply and sanitation.
- Ensure the efficiency and financial sustainability of water and wastewater operations.
- Increase investment attractiveness of the water sector and maximise involvement of private capital in the financing of water and sanitation projects.
- Maximise the potential of using groundwater for drinking water supply.
- Improve the design of water and wastewater infrastructure.
- Create a system for monitoring water and sanitation sector.
- Create a system for monitoring groundwater and surface water quality.
- Ensure that water tariffs are sufficient for the sustainable operation of water management organisations, making sure that long-term and cost-effective tariffs guarantee a return on investment.
- Reduce non-revenue water during transport to the consumer to a technically appropriate level.
- Develop local content in designing water and sanitation projects.

For 2011-20, the Ak Bulak Programme was projected to cost KZT 1 273.8 bn (KZT 1 164.1 bn from the central budget and KZT 109.7 bn from local budgets).

Source: Ak Bulak Programme.

Data on the current status of WSS services in rural areas show that significant progress is necessary to reach the Ak Bulak objectives. Success requires not only mobilisation of financial and human resources, but also the development of WSS projects ready for implementation. The recent shortage of new WSS projects is caused by the following factors:

- delay in exploration and confirmation of groundwater resources

In 2012, the Ministry of Industry and New Technologies launched the exploration of groundwater resources for 341 villages, which was completed in late 2013. As a result, the programme has been adjusted, and target indicators reduced, thus increasing the scope of work in the second phase. In 2013, groundwater exploration began for only 216 of 480 planned villages. This caused further delays in implementation and jeopardises the realisation of the Ak Bulak objectives in general.

- delay in construction and rehabilitation of grouped water mains

In light of the various delays, and in order to improve implementation, the following recommendations were made by experts:

- Implementation should first focus on providing access to centralised drinking water systems in large populated areas.
- The use of local water resources should be prioritised, and standard engineering designs for areas with small populations should be developed and disseminated.
- Groundwater exploration and validation should be assigned to local authorities.

- Insufficient allocation of funds by local authorities for the design of WSS systems and the Bill of Quantities (BOQ) estimates.

An analysis of the Drinking Water and Ak Bulak programmes shows that many newly-constructed WSS systems do not function adequately due to the absence of unified technical standards and the use of poor quality materials. To improve quality of design and construction, the Ministry adopted a special procedure for the development, co-ordination and approval of engineering documentation for the construction of WSS infrastructure. It will help regulate the quality of materials, equipment and technologies at all stages, from design to construction and commissioning.

Another acute problem is unsustainability, or the lack, of operators of newly built or rehabilitated WSS systems in rural settlements.

A single (national) operator to manage drinking water and sanitation services in rural areas was proposed to solve such complex problems as poor planning, design and construction, as well as the lack, or unsustainability, of organisations in charge of operation and maintenance. It was assumed this strategy would provide i) a more efficient, centralised management of WSS in rural areas; and ii) a uniform approach to planning, designing, constructing and operating the WSS infrastructure that would accommodate future forms of PPP.

Recognising the importance of private sector participation, the government adopted on 29 June 2011, Resolution No.731: On the Approval of the Development of Public-Private Partnerships (PPPs) in the Republic of Kazakhstan for 2011-15. In 2011, the Ministry of Agriculture developed a procedure for introducing PPPs in the construction of drinking water facilities in rural areas. The aim was threefold: increase effectiveness and efficiency of WSS operations; reduce the burden on the national and local budgets; and increase access to drinking water and sanitation services in urban and rural areas. The main prerequisite for increasing investments from the private sector is the profitability of WSS services, which should guarantee a return on investments. The policy is contingent upon finding the right balance between sustainable cost recovery and affordability of water tariffs. The Agency on Architecture, Housing and Utilities with the support of the European Bank for Reconstruction and Development (EBRD) has already developed a pilot project to attract private investment to WSS in the cities of Semey, Taraz and Atyrau.

Endnotes

[1]The administrative and territorial organisation of Kazakhstan is regulated by the Law on Administrative–Territorial Division of the Republic of Kazakhstan No. 2572-XII, adopted on 8 December 1993.

[2]In 2004, the total number of rural communities was 7 511. In 2010, there were only 7 002 rural communities, as a result of the government's administrative-territorial policy and programmes.

[3]There are 86 cities in Kazakhstan with a total of about 9 436 900 residents: three cities with a population exceeding 500 000 (including one city with over 1 mln residents), 18 cities with between 100 000 and 500 000 residents, 6 cities with between 50 000 and 100 000 residents, and 59 small cities (towns) with a population under 50 000 residents (hereinafter referred to as small towns).

[4]http://stats.oecd.org/

[5]OECD Environment Statistics

[6]www.stat.gov.kz

[7]In OECD member countries, the average domestic consumption is approximately 180 litres per capita per day. *Source*: www.oecd.stat.

[8]The low levels of water losses should be subject to further analysis to confirm the accuracy of the data, as these estimates do not correspond to the fact that around 65% of WSS systems are in critical condition and require rehabilitation.

[9] Water tariffs are regulated by the Agency for Regulation of Natural Monopolies of the Republic of Kazakhstan, which acts in accordance with the Law of the Republic of Kazakhstan dated July 9, 1998, No. 272-I: On Natural Monopolies and Regulated Markets. The methodology used for calculating water tariffs is outlined in Methodology for the Calculation of Differentiated Tariffs for Regulated Services of Water and Sewerage Systems, approved by the order of the Chairman of Agency for Regulation of Natural Monopolies on December 30, 2009, No. 419-OD. The legal framework regulating this activity includes the following acts:

- decree of the President of the Republic of Kazakhstan dated March 19, 2010, No. 58: On the State Program to Strengthen the Industrial and Innovative Development of Kazakhstan for 2010-14
- resolution of the Government of the Republic of Kazakhstan of September 30, 2010, No. 1005: On the Approval of the Tariff Policy of the Republic of Kazakhstan for 2010-14
- resolution of the Government of the Republic of Kazakhstan dated December 29, 2012, No. 1779: On the Approval of the Comprehensive Plan for the Introduction of Mechanisms for Water Tariffs in the Republic of Kazakhstan for 2013-15.

References

OECD (2003), *Social Issues in the Provision and Pricing of Water Services*, OECD Publishing, Paris.
http://dx.doi.org/10.1787/9789264099890-en

Can Poor Consumers Pay for Energy and Water? An Affordability Analysis for Transition Countries. Samuel Fankhauser and Sladjana Tepic, EBRD Working Paper No. 92 (2005).
http://www.ebrd.com/downloads/research/economics/workingpapers/wp0092.pdf

Chapter 2.

Prevailing Business Models for Water Supply and Sanitation in Small Towns and Rural Areas in Kazakhstan

This section discusses existing WSS business models in small towns and rural areas in Kazakhstan. As official data on the legal and institutional organisation of WSS operators were not available, the information presented here is based on the knowledge and experience of local project experts.

The existing WSS business models in small towns and rural areas in Kazakhstan are the following:

- *a large farm or an agricultural enterprise*[1]
- *a small town water utility*
- *a multi-services utility*
- *a rayon water utility*
- *grouped water mains as a source of water*
- *an individual private operator under a service contract or lease or concession agreement (public-private partnership model)*
- *a community-based organisation (e.g. rural consumer co-operatives).*

According to national experts, large farm or individual private operators that provide WSS services are the main model of service delivery in many small towns and villages (representing about 61% of the total rural population). Small town water utilities, including multi-services utility and rayon water utility, service around 33% of the rural population. Community-based organisations serve only 6% of the rural population.

WSS service delivery model: Large farm or agricultural enterprise

Usually, large farms or agricultural enterprises rely on their own WSS systems and have their own operation and maintenance personnel. In the case of more complex operations, they contract out engineering services to private companies. The farms usually provide drinking water for their own needs and for the household needs of their employees free of charge. If they are selling water to other consumers, they may charge a water tariff approved by the Agency of Regulating Natural Monopolies (AREM).

There are no available official data on the percentage of rural population served by the model of large farm and agriculture enterprises. According to national experts, however, this model is one of the most prevalent in rural areas. Together with small private operators, it delivers WSS services to about half of the rural population, especially in the eastern and northern regions. Local authorities support this model because it does not require any allocation of public funds from local budgets. Consequently, local authorities often turn to the farms and to agricultural enterprises with requests to operate existing public WSS infrastructure. But since farmers and agricultural enterprises have no expertise in delivering WSS services other than for their own needs, this often results in inadequate water supply and sanitation service delivery. Inadequate operation and maintenance leads to frequent technical failures and breakdowns, and irregular water delivery. Besides technical problems, there are also legal issues associated with this model; local authorities usually do not provide big farms and agricultural companies with appropriate legal and technical documentation to operate and maintain WSS infrastructure. In principle, these suppliers should have a lease or concession contract with local authorities. In practice, these arrangements are rare as the legal framework for small-scale private-public partnerships (PPPs) is not fully developed.

WSS service delivery model: Small town water utility

Small town water utilities are generally established by the local authorities of rayons and, sometimes, of oblasts.[2] Water utilities can be established as state-run enterprises or commercial companies (limited liability companies or joint stock companies). Local authorities generally own commercial companies, although there are some examples of mixed public and private ownership more common in mid-sized and large cities. Usually, the water utility provides both drinking water and sanitation services. In rare cases, it provides a so-called multi-service communal enterprise/utility (see section IV.6). The WSS services are financed by the customers' payments of water tariffs. Because small towns often do not have enough customers to finance the full cost of WSS services, water utilities in search of additional customers might consider extending their WSS infrastructure to surrounding settlements. This option is fully in line with the regionalisation policy and can provide many benefits, both for the water utility and for consumers in the surrounding settlements (see Box 2.1).

Box 2.1. Water utility in the town of Talgar expands its service area to surrounding settlements

The town of Talgar (pop. 45 529) is located in Talgar Rayon (pop. 156 940, area 3 700 km2, density 42.41 people/km2) in Almaty Oblast. The rayon authorities established a state communal enterprise Vodocanal, which delivered WSS services in Talgar. Recently, rayon authorities have been working on re-registering the Vodocanal under the new name of Su Kubyry, with a new service area, extending services to settlements near Talgar. The sustainability of this model depends on achieving a balance between the principle of full cost recovery from water tariffs and their affordability for the population.

Source: Author's own assessment based on information from rayon administration.

Given the low population density in Kazakhstan, the small town water utility model is not a solution for all rural areas. Small towns often do not provide sufficient population density and economic activity for viable centralised (piped) WSS; such systems often struggle with low financial sustainability, as well as lack of technical capacity.

WSS service delivery model: Rayon water utility

According to national experts, rayon water utilities service about 15% of the rural population. The Ak Bulak programme, which promotes this model of WSS service delivery, assumes that each rayon in the country will form a water utility. Although this model looks promising, each rayon will require a feasibility assessment, especially considering the country's low population density. The model can only operate where full cost recovery from water tariffs is balanced with affordability for the local population. Additional studies for specific rayons should determine the economic feasibility of the current and future service area of a rayon water utility. Areas outside the service area will need to be served by other models.

A rayon water utility often owns several separate centralised WSS systems. In such cases, water tariffs are individually calculated for each centralised WSS system; overhead costs are apportioned between the services through a specific cost-sharing formula. Another option is to have a single tariff for the entire service area; in this case, tariffs collected from the urban population are used to cross-subsidise WSS services for the rural population (Box 2.2).

Box 2.2. Rayon water utility in the village of Chundzha, Uygur Rayon, Almaty Oblast

Uygur Rayon (pop. 64 762, area 8 700 km, density 7.44 people/km2) includes 14 rural districts and 25 small towns. The rayon water utility, a state communal enterprise called Uygyr Su Kubyry, was created by the authorities of Uygur Rayon to provide WSS services. It services seven villages, or about 48% of the rayon population (31 085 people):

- Chundzha, pop.18 500, length of WSS network 73.6 km
- Bakhar, pop. 1 500, length of WSS network 9.1 km
- Taskarasu, pop. 3 200, length of WSS network 15.5 km
- Sunkar, pop. 1800, length of WSS network 12.5 km
- Ketmen, pop. 2 600, length of WSS network 20.6 km
- Tigermen, pop. 2 600, length of WSS network 18.3 km
- Shirin, pop. 1 200, length of WSS network 6.5 km.

After implementation of the Ak Bulak Programme, the number of settlements covered by the utility will increase. The rayon water utility owns the WSS network; the Department of the Agency for Regulation of Natural Monopolies of Almaty Oblast approves water tariffs. The rates depend on the water source and range from an average of KZT 30 to KZT 43 per m3; water consumption ranges from 50 to 180 lcd. Local employees of the rayon utility operate the local WSS networks; their number ranges between three to five people in each settlement, depending on the length of the network. The sustainability of this interesting model of WSS service delivery depends on achieving a balance between full cost recovery from water tariffs and affordability for the local population.

Source : Interviews with managers of Uygyr Su Kubyry Regional WSS utility.

WSS service delivery model: Grouped water mains

Areas with no water sources of their own have to rely on piped water delivered from distant water sources by grouped water mains This model is operated by the Republican State Enterprise (RSE) Kazvodhoz, which in 2014 was subordinated to the Committee of Water Resources under the Ministry of Environment and Water Resources. RSE Kazvodhoz has local branches in each oblast and in the two major cities of Astana and Almaty, as well as specialised and "thematic" branches (Aral, Yesil Su, Ontustikauyzsu and Su Metrology).

These local branches own the grouped water mains. The list of grouped water mains, approved by the government in Resolution No 1265 of 13 December 2003, comprises 304 objects, including 45 grouped systems. Resolution No 248 of 5 April 2006 approved rules for subsidising the cost of drinking water from the grouped water mains, where those are the only source of drinking water.

The local branches of RSE Kazvodhoz operate and maintain grouped water mains, and deliver water to local WSS systems. An agreement stipulates the rights and obligations of each party; it designates the location where the responsibility of RSE Kazvodhoz ends and the responsibility of local WSS operators starts.

WSS service delivery model: Multi-service utility

In searching for a way to provide sustainable WSS services, local authorities have also considered multi-service utilities, as well as the regionalisation of WSS services. In Kazakhstan, there are 59 urban settlements with populations below 50 000 residents; those are formally called small towns. Forty-one of those (i.e. 68% of small towns) are administrative centres of their respective rayons.[3] The total population of small towns is more than 1.5 mln people, or 8.8% of the total population of Kazakhstan. In terms of population size, 13 small towns have fewer than 10 000 residents.[4] At the same time, as the size of population is not the only criterion for assigning the status of "town", many rural settlements in Kazakhstan with populations ranging between 10 000 to 20 000 people do not fall under the small town category.

The model of WSS delivery by multi-service utility is often found in small towns, where population density and economic activity is low. One of the solutions for decreasing unit costs of WSS service delivery is to share overhead costs between different utility services. WSS services, district heating (DH) services and other communal services, for example, can pool management, administrative and financial functions. Typically, multi-service utilities provide the following services:

- thermal energy generation, transfer and distribution, O&M, and capital repairs of enterprises' and institutions' heating networks
- water supply and sanitation services, O&M and capital repairs of enterprises' and institutions' water supply and sanitation networks
- bulk purchase of electricity, its transportation, distribution and sale to end-users through transformer sub-stations, high-voltage and low-voltage distribution networks, O&M capital repairs of enterprises' and institutions' electric networks
- bulk purchase of natural gas, O&M and capital repairs of gas pipelines and gas distribution points
- municipal waste management
- O&M and capital repairs of control and measuring devices, installation of utility meters for users
- service provision by motor vehicles and devices.

Small town multi-service utilities typically function as state-owned utilities or limited liability companies. Groundwater and surface water (from rivers with natural or regulated flow, as well as from water reservoirs) are used as sources of water supply. Many towns have no centralised sanitation systems; existing wastewater treatment plants are either non-existent, used well below their design capacity and/or fail to perform up to established requirements/treatment standards.

WSS service delivery by individual private operator under a service contract, lease or concession contracts (PPP model)

According to Article 27 of the Water Code, the WSS infrastructure can be subject to free use, trust management or lease by a private entity, with the exception of strategically important objects if it is communal property and owned by a state communal enterprise.

Based on this, rayon authorities may choose not to establish their own water utilities, but rather sign an agreement with a private operator to operate and maintain WSS infrastructure and deliver WSS services. The agreement should be made through a public tender that selects the bid offering the best value. According to the Agency of Statistics of the Republic of Kazakhstan, only eight lease and concession contracts have been signed in rural areas. According to national experts, the lack of experience in applying lease and concession contracts in small WSS supply systems is one factor influencing the small uptake of such models in rural areas in Kazakhstan. Other factors are the lack of WSS infrastructure and its poor condition, which may not seem attractive enough to the private sector, as well as small consumer base in rural areas. In this situation, development of this model will require a solid legal base and consolidations of small local markets in bigger ones that are more attractive for the private sector.

WSS service delivery model: Community-based organisation

According to national experts, only about 6% of the rural population is served by this model in Kazakhstan. Experts believe that establishing water user co-operatives requires mobilisation of the local community, which is not easy and not popular with local authorities. There are still some expectations that WSS services should be organised by public authorities, not by communities themselves. Although not very popular in Kazakhstan, the community management model is very important for ensuring WSS services in many rural areas. This is especially true in areas with low population density and lower levels of economic activity, which do not allow the development of other forms of organisation. International experience shows this model requires significant efforts to develop community capacity along with an effective system of external backup assistance to ensure long-term sustainability.

In Kazakhstan, the model of community management of WSS services takes the form of **rural consumer co-operatives.**[5] According to the law, a rural consumer co-operative is a voluntary association of citizens on the basis of membership established by combining property and financial contributions. **Members of the rural water user co-operative may be both physical persons and legal entities**. Local authorities have no right to interfere in the economic, financial and other activities of rural consumer co-operatives. Figure 3 presents the procedure for forming a rural water user co-operative.

Figure 2.1. Process of forming a rural water user co-operative

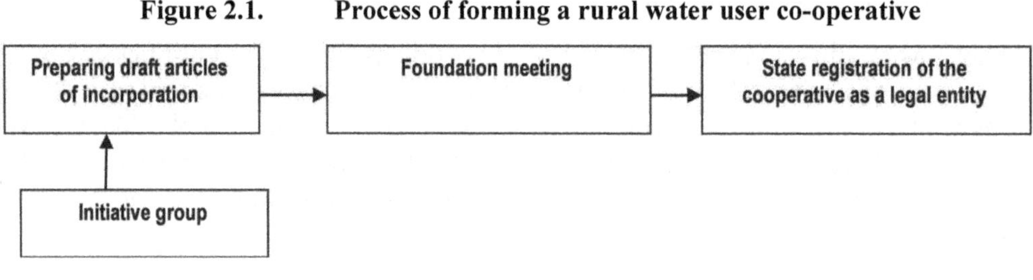

Source: Authors' own findings.

Figure 2.2 presents the overall management structure of a rural water user co-operative.

Figure 2.2. Management structure of a rural water user co-operative

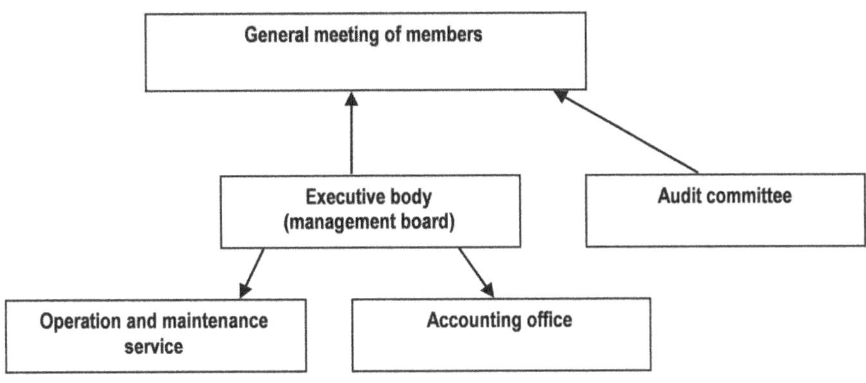

Source: Authors' own findings.

A rural water user co-operative establishes its own services for the operation and maintenance of WSS infrastructure. In the case of a small rural settlement, it usually consists of one technician only; a larger system may have a few technicians. In the case of a complex system, a rural water user co-operative may choose to contract out operations and maintenance to an external private company (outsourcing). **The law allows for creating a rural water user co-operative not only for one rural settlement, but also for two or more settlements**. In this case, one co-operative delivers WSS services to several rural settlements. Under this model, all expenses are financed by contributions of water users; tariffs or monthly fees cover the cost of operation and maintenance of respective WSS systems. Box 2.3 illustrates two examples of projects on developing community management of WSS service delivery in rural settlements in Kazakhstan.

Box 2.3. Project implemented by UNDP and Coca-Cola company in Almaty Oblast, Karasay Rayon

The objective of the project was to rehabilitate WSS infrastructure in the village of Kok Ozek to ensure the delivery of WSS services to the population of the village (2 500 people). The project stakeholders were the following:

- the local authorities of Karasay Rayon and the village of Kok Ozek, responsible for developing technical designs and cost estimation documents,
- the Coca-Cola Company, responsible for financing the rehabilitation of the water well and the construction of main water pipes in the streets of the village,
- the population of the village of Kok Ozek, which contributed in kind to the project, through labour and construction work by connecting their homes to the main water pipes in the streets, and
- the UNDP, responsible for the funding of community mobilisation activities and establishing and registering the water user co-operative.

The established rural water user cooperative includes the following bodies:

- the general assembly, which is the highest governing body of the co-operative,
- the board, which is the executive body of the co-operative,
- the audit commission, which is the supervisory body of the co-operative,
- the O&M Service, responsible for O&M and repair of WSS infrastructure, and
- the accounting department, responsible for financial management of the co-operative.

The co-operative employs one person to operate and maintain WSS infrastructure. It provides only drinking water services because there is no sewerage system in the village; each household has a septic tank. Although this could be considered an example of a successful rural water user co-operative, one challenge remains: the constructed WSS infrastructure assets, which were handed over to the co-operative, are not officially registered with the co-operative, and there are no detailed technical documents for the infrastructure. This is linked to the significant costs of developing technical documentation. Another issue is that sustainability of the co-operative requires continuous external support and assistance.

Source : Author's own assessment based on information provided by the UNDP.

Box 2.4 illustrates an example of another project, implemented between 2003-10.

Box 2.4. The Clean Water for Rural Communities in Kazakhstan project implemented by the Regional Environment Centre for Central Asia in Almaty Oblast

The Clean Water for Rural Communities in Kazakhstan project was financed by the European Commission, the governments of Norway and the United States, and the Ministry of Foreign Affairs of Germany through GIZ. The project was implemented by the Regional Environmental Centre for Central Asia in 2003-10. The first phase took place in Almaty Oblast; subsequent phases entail scaling up the project, first in the territory of Kazakhstan and then in other Central Asian countries. The project began in rural settlements with populations under 1 000 people that were not included in the State Drinking Water Programme. In Almaty Oblast, the following villages were selected:

- Algabas
- Tenlik
- "1st of May"
- Kopberlik
- Beskaynar
- Konyr
- "10 years of Kazakhstan"
- Kyzyltogan
- Enbekshikazah
- Mukri
- Keneral
- Maulenbay.

One of the main objectives was to achieve sustainability of WSS operations and maintenance, while ensuring the quality of WSS services to the population. This was supposed to be achieved through mobilisation of the local population and creation of rural water user co-operatives, in partnership with local authorities. It was assumed the local population would contribute financially to operations and maintenance of WSS infrastructure via water tariffs consistent with the cost recovery principle. Furthermore, the project assumed that stakeholders would finance the total cost of rehabilitation and construction work as follows:

- 70% from donors
- 20% from local authorities
- 10% from the population of beneficiary villages.

Simultaneously, the project worked on establishing and building the capacity of rural water co-operatives, which were benefiting from the constructed infrastructure. In 2009-10, the Regional Environmental Centre for Central Asia (CAREC) in co-operation with the Committee on Water Resources of the Ministry of Agriculture and the rayon Akimats implemented the second phase of the project. The second phase sought primarily to showcase the experience of the first phase and to scale it up for the whole territory of Kazakhstan. It organised 14 regional and national conferences to share the experience of solving the drinking water problem in Almaty Oblast. The project did not find much support among local authorities from other oblasts because creating a rural water user co-operative requires significant efforts and costs. In this regard, the objectives of the second phase of the project were not achieved.

Source: Author's own assessment based on information from CAREC.

Prevailing WSS business models: Lessons learned for Kazakhstan

Sustainable access to safe drinking water and appropriate sanitation are among the key objectives of the Millennium Development Goals (MDGs) and a key pillar of Kazakhstan's transition to a green economy. In this regard, **Kazakhstan has undertaken significant measures to develop WSS services in the entire country**. Within the framework of the Drinking Water Programme and now Ak Bulak Programme, significant public funds have been allocated for construction and rehabilitation of WSS infrastructure. In addition, regional and rural development initiatives have accompanied WSS development initiatives aimed at improving living conditions, especially in rural areas. A water tariff policy to improve the effectiveness and efficiency of the WSS sector has recently enhanced investments. **However, much remains to be done to ensure sustainable WSS service delivery, especially in small towns and rural areas.**

The review of the prevailing WSS business models in Kazakhstan highlights **the lack of a systematic approach to institutional development of WSS in small towns and rural areas**. Together with the low population density and economic activity in small towns and rural areas, the business models result in weak institutional structures and low sustainability of WSS service delivery. These need to be addressed as part of the WSS development programme.

Lessons learned from Kazakhstan and other countries (see Annexes A-B) suggest it is insufficient simply to rehabilitate or build new infrastructure to improve the quality of WSS services. It is also necessary to develop organisational, managerial, technical and financial capacity to ensure sustainable operations, maintenance and financing of WSS systems. This is especially important in the development and rehabilitation of WSS infrastructure in small towns and rural areas, where the issue of sustainable business models for proper operations, maintenance and financing of the newly developed WSS infrastructure requires special attention.

Table 2.1 provides a summary of benefits and drawbacks of prevailing WSS business models in Kazakhstan, as well as possible improvements for building long-term sustainability.

Table 2.1. The main benefits and drawbacks of the prevailing business models in small towns and rural areas in Kazakhstan

Prevailing WSS business model	Benefits	Drawbacks	Possible improvements of existing business model
Model of a large farm or agricultural enterprise	Possibility of using WSS infrastructure of large farms for supplying WSS services to surrounding households	Lack of necessary human capacity for provision of WSS services to the entire rural community	Only applicable for self-supply of WSS services for the own needs of large farms
Model of WSS service delivery by a community- based organisation	Delivering of WSS services by the community itself	Lack of necessary human capacity for delivering WSS services; need for continuous external assistance	Providing external assistance and specialised services
Model of WSS service delivery by a small town water utility	Providing quality WSS services to the population of a small town	Revenue from the small client base is not sufficient to cover all costs in service delivery and extension	Regionalisation
Model of WSS service delivery by a rayon water utility	Providing quality WSS services to urban territories within rayon	Requiring time and investments in building the needed structures	Incorporation of companies/utilities
Model of grouped water mains	Providing a source of water for communities without their own sources	Large investments and higher cost of water	Subsidising costs of water transportation
Model of multi-service utility (WSS and district heating [DH])	Sharing a pool of technicians and overhead costs between services	Unintended cross-subsidisation	Regionalisation
Model of WSS service delivery under a service contract, lease or concession contracts (PPP model)	Using private know-how for delivering WSS services	Lack of experience and conducive regulatory framework	Building experience in PPP arrangements based on a more conducive legal, institutional and regulatory framework

Source: Author's own assessment

Rural areas currently do not provide the most optimal conditions for WSS institutional development. The prevailing WSS business model in rural areas in Kazakhstan is the large farm or individual private operator. Both models have their roots in the *kolkhoz-sovkhoz* system, which was also responsible for rural social infrastructure, including centralised water supply systems in local communities. With liquidation of the *kolkhoz-sovkhoz* system, the infrastructure was initially transferred to local public administrations and then often to newly created farms or individual private operators; however, this process was a result of local circumstances and not adequately planned. Without a systematic approach, local authorities continue to co-operate with the two models, often without the support of licences or management and concession contracts; however, they have no other alternative.

The **large farm or agriculture enterprise model** may be an adequate option for self-supply or servicing surrounding households, but not for rural communities as a whole. A recommended alternative is community-based management, where the community itself is responsible for managing WSS services. The main drawback of this business model is the lack of the necessary human capacity for the provision of WSS services; this can be developed through external technical assistance and specialised services.

Although the **first water user co-operatives** were established several years ago in rural Kazakhstan, the community management model of WSS services is still not widely used, regardless of its benefits for the rural population. Apart from legal, technical and financial issues (such as the high costs of making an inventory of existing WSS infrastructure), there are also social issues to consider in promoting and scaling up this model. Furthermore, mobilising local communities and strengthening village authorities is critical to build sustainability of WSS service delivery in rural areas.

In small towns, the small town water utility, or the multi-service utility, is the prevailing WSS business model in general. The **small town water utility** model does not address the challenge of a small WSS client base; if not subsidised, utility operations may not be financially sustainable.

To address this challenge, local authorities may also consider the model of the **multi-service utility**, e.g. combining WSS services with district heating (DH) services. Although both are infrastructure services, the synergies between the two have gone largely undeveloped. Multi-service utilities can benefit from sharing overhead costs and using the same pool of equipment and technicians, for example, thus addressing the human capacity constraints typical of small settlements. In theory, the approach works, but in practice, it creates a **risk of hidden (unintended) and non-transparent cross-subsidies between the services.** In this case, consolidation and regionalisation is the recommended option, but this requires a rayon for the required optimal scale. International experience also shows that voluntary consolidation and regionalisation is not an easy process for addressing a fragmented WSS institutional setup, which resulted from earlier decentralisation. As a result, the process needs to be either centrally managed, or implemented together with a significant incentive package.

In small towns, another possible and existing business model is the water utility that also delivers WSS services in neighbouring villages. In this case, the small size of the customer base is both an advantage and disadvantage: it allows for the provision of good quality WSS services, but usually does not generate enough revenue to cover the full costs of service delivery and extension.

The **WSS sector regionalisation process** may help address this challenge: in this model, WSS service delivery is in the hands of rayon water utilities, which service settlements within a given rayon. This solution requires time and investments to build the required structures; it can be improved by incorporating public utilities.

An additional complementary WSS business model is that of **grouped water mains**, which enables the delivery of water to communities that lack local water sources. However, large investments are needed for this business model, which results in a higher cost of water overall. Subsidising water transportation costs might be the only way to ensure sustainability.

Finally, a promising WSS business model for small towns and rural settlements is the private operator model (including small-scale and local private sector) working under management, lease or concession contracts (i.e. the PPP model). The main benefit of the

PPP model is the opportunity to use private know-how for delivering WSS services; its main drawback is the need for a strong regulatory framework, as well as a suitably sized market of private operators.

Despite significant efforts to obtain data on WSS services in small towns and rural areas, the required information is not accessible. This presents a major obstacle for designing sound programmes for rural WSS development. Addressing this issue would require additional efforts to create a system for continuous monitoring of institutional development and performance of the WSS sector in small towns and rural areas.

Endnotes

[1]In fact, the WSS business model of big farm and agriculture enterprise should be classified as the model of private operator under PPP contract, but as it has its own specific characteristics in the Kazakhstan environment it is presented here as a separate business model.

[2]The legal basis for this is Section Five of the Law of the Republic of Kazakhstan: On State Property.

[3]One city, Baikonur, leased by the Russian Federation, has a special status: the Kazakh authorities record it as an oblast city as part of Kyzylorda Oblast.

[4]*Zhem* with a population of 1 942 persons is the smallest town.

[5]The legal basis for the establishment and operations of the rural water user co-operatives is the Law of the Republic of Kazakhstan dated July 21, 1999, No. 450–I: On Rural Consumer Co-operatives in the Republic of Kazakhstan.

Chapter 3.

Recommended business models for Water Supply and Sanitation in Kazakhstan

Due to the low population density in Kazakhstan, individual (servicing just one household) WSS systems will be used in many small and remote villages. Only areas with sufficient density of population and of economic activity are or could be served by centralised (piped) WSS systems requiring professional operators. For such areas, the key recommended WSS business model is the Rayon Vodocanal model; while other communities might have to use alternative business models that can complement the Rayon Vodocanal model, such as: service delivery by community-based organisations (CBOs) or by small-scale private operators or by multi-service utilities (typically in towns). All these models are discussed below, one by one. The proposed Rayon WSS Master Plan should help define the communities that will be included in the service area of the Rayon Vodocanal, and those that will be served by other complementary models, back-stopped by the Rayon Vodocanal.

Rayon Vodocanal business model

Rayon Vodocanal is a water utility with the mandate to provide WSS services to the whole rayon or even to an area larger than one rayon (in case of inter-rayonal co-operation). The Rayon Vodocanal operates in several municipalities and settlements (including towns and villages). In such large areas, it is difficult to have only one centralised WSS system; in most cases, the Rayon Vodocanal will operate several independent centralised WSS systems, mainly in urban centres and perhaps extended to the surrounding rural areas. The benefit of the Rayon Vodocanal relates to the possibility of achieving economies of scale when merging smaller service areas together, and improving cost efficiency by centralising management, maintenance and backstopping functions.

Rayon Vodocanals can be created by merging and reorganising existing water utilities based in small towns through centralised management functions and decentralised operations. It is recommended that Rayon Vodocanals are incorporated as a company; limited liability companies are the preferred legal form for Rayon Vodocanals given the conditions in rural Kazakhstan. The initial capital of Rayon Vodocanals will consist of the assets of the water utilities being merged. An updated inventory and formal evaluation of the WSS assets will be needed for declaring the Vodocanals' charter capital.

The Rayon Vodocanal will be fully owned by the respective rayon administration. Depending on local conditions, the merged water utilities may function as local branches of the Rayon Vodocanal or may be centres of operations. Management functions, including human resources and financial management, administration and other auxiliary functions, will be centralised in the main office of the Rayon Vodocanal. Operational functions related to WSS service delivery will be provided locally, based on the local infrastructure of the former water utilities of small towns and large villages.

Although the Rayon Vodocanal will own and operate centralised WSS systems mainly in urban centres, it might be obliged to provide supporting services to community-managed WSS systems within the administrative territory of respective rayons. These may include laboratory services like checking quality of drinking water, repair of water pipes and pumps, sanitation services like collecting wastewater and sludge from individual septic tanks, transport of wastewater to a treatment plant, etc. These services are very important for the sustainability of alternative WSS business models in communities not served directly by the Rayon Vodocanal. It is important that the various functions of Rayon Vodocanals are included in its statutes.

Similar to a limited liability company, the Rayon Vodocanal has a management and a supervisory board. It is recommended that members of the supervisory board are representatives of the communities served by the Rayon Vodocanal.

When creating Rayon Vodocanals, prior to making a final decision, a financial analysis should confirm the proposed structure will be financially sustainable. Considering the conditions of small towns and rural areas in Kazakhstan, including the low population density and low level of development of centralised WSS systems, Rayon Vodocanals will likely need a support programme for strengthening their capacity and financial sustainability.

Business model of community-based organisation for WSS services delivery

Rayon Vodocanals cannot be the sole and only business model for WSS services delivery in many rural areas; a complementary model is the **community-based organisation (CBO).** Community-managed, decentralised water supply systems are found to be quite successful in providing sustainable water supply services for rural communities, given they receive sufficient back-stopping technical support. Their basic characteristics are the following:

- Water sources should be located close to the community.
- CBOs (also known in Kazakhstan as water user co-operatives) should manage the WSS system.
- Communities should be highly involved during the construction, operation and maintenance of the system.
- The infrastructure is generally owned by local authorities, which grant operational concessions to water user co-operatives (in some cases, the co-operative may own fixed WSS assets).

The principle of mandating CBOs for the operations and management of WSS services is to put citizens in the centre of the management of small centralised WSS systems. Their participation throughout building, operating, maintaining and co-financing the system in their own community creates ownership, thus contributing to the sustainability of WSS services. The CBOs will need assistance in constructing their centralised WSS systems; as a general rule, local authorities provide investments with some small contribution from citizens, mainly related to financing households' connections.

The organisational structure of CBOs includes regular general meetings, a management board and service staff, including an accountant. The general meeting involves all members of the water user co-operative; it has the authority to adopt a plan of work and water tariffs, as well as appoint the management board. The management board organises the work of the respective water user co-operative and makes operational decisions. Technical staff takes care of operations; generally, just one person is responsible for technical operations of a small WSS system; accounting is another important function. **Water user co-operatives are non-profit organisations**, meaning that any revenue generated by operations is used to maintain, develop or rehabilitate WSS systems.

Alternative WSS business models: Multi-service utilities and small-scale private operators

A multi-service utility is by definition a single company providing several utility services, including (but not restricted to) water supply and wastewater services. The model is widely used in some EECCA countries, notably in the Russian Federation and Ukraine. It is also present in other places in Western Europe (such as Germany and Italy) and in Central Europe (such as Serbia, Poland and Hungary), particularly in small municipalities. These multi-service utilities provide different types of municipal services, such as water supply and wastewater collection and treatment, district heating, municipal waste management, street cleaning, urban green space management, and housing management and maintenance. In Italy, in addition to the above, multi-service utilities provide gas and electricity distribution services. The advantage of a multi-service utility lies in its larger scope and scale, which enables it to cover overhead and maintenance costs from different sources, not only from water and wastewater services.

On the other hand, multi-service utilities have some disadvantages, which is why many countries do not use them. A major challenge is related to the proper allocation of costs attributed to different services, which requires enhanced accounting skills and information technology. In another disadvantage, which reduces the applicability of the model in Kazakhstan, it is not always possible to provide other public services in combination with water supply and wastewater. For example, district heating, urban green space management and street cleansing, and housing management and maintenance are organised in larger towns only. Furthermore, the optimal size of the service areas might be very different for different utility services. This model can still be applied, even with different service areas, but needs to be carefully considered prior to implementation.

Another alternative WSS business model that could be used in rural areas is the private operator model, typically small-scale. Currently, many small private operators deliver WSS services in rural areas in Kazakhstan. However, these operators often do not have the full legal rights to provide WSS services; local authorities are aware of this, but no measures are taken as they do not have any alternative. If the involvement of small private operators in the WSS sector can be formalised, the model could become a viable option for rural areas.

Retaining small private operators to provide WSS services is more advantageous in two cases:

- Private operators have better access to water sources or to specific WSS infrastructure (e.g. WWTP).
- Private operators have built and operated small-scale facilities (e.g. WTP or WWTP) locally, and provide in-house professional maintenance services.

Complementarity of proposed business models

A summary on the complementarity of recommended WSS business models for small towns and rural areas in Kazakhstan is presented in Table 9 below. The main recommended WSS business model is the Rayon Vodocanal, which can be a standalone model or complemented by other models more suitable for remote small rural communities, like community-managed WSS or small private operator. The Rayon Vodocanal needs to offer specialised backup services to these two complementary models to ensure they are technically sustainable. In this way, all the models complement each other: the Rayon Vodocanal will sell its expertise and engineering services, while the community-managed WSS or small private operator will serve rural communities that the Rayon Vodoncanal cannot service because they are either too small (to provide a profitable customer base) or too far away (which makes its services too costly).

In addition, Table 3.1 presents the model of multi-service utility that helps achieve economies of scale by providing other communal services together with WSS services.

Table 3.1.Complementarity of proposed business models

Business model	Service area	Degree of regionalisation	Legal form of service provision	Professional back-up services	Complementarity to other business models
Rayon Vodocanal	Rayon (or a large part of it; or several neighbouring rayons)	Regionalised	Limited liability or joint stock company	Provided in-house	Could be a standalone model or complemented by other business models used in some settlements
Community-based organisation	One settlement, or a group of neighbouring settlements	Decentralised	Community-based organisation	Provided by Rayon Vodocanal	Limited to remotely located settlements, co-exists well with Rayon Vodocanal which shall provide professional backstopping services to CBOs
Private operator(small-scale)	One settlement, or a group of neighbouring settlements	Decentralised	Private	Some (like lab test) provided by Rayon Vodocanal, but some provided in-house	Limited to remotely located settlements Can co-exist with other models
Multi-service utility	Single town, or rayon (or a large part of it)	Regionalised or operating in any specific town	Limited liability or Joint stock company	Provided in-house	Can co-exist with other models

Source: Authors' own work.

Towards an action plan on implementing the recommended WSS business models

The recommended Rayon Vodocanal business model assumes the rayon administration organises WSS service provision on its territory by establishing Rayon Vodocanals. In addition to deliver WSS services on the territory of rayon, Rayon Vodocanals will also facilitate and support complementary business models, where needed.

The Rayon WSS Development Plan (Master Plan), which should be prepared and approved by the rayon administration, outlines specific arrangements. In addition to engineering designs for WSS infrastructure, the plan should analyse a variety of WSS business models and select those that best suit local hydrological, engineering, financial and social conditions. It must outline the proposed WSS business models at the local level and their respective service areas in the mid- and long-term. The plan should indicate which areas will have to rely on self-supply of WSS services, those which are or will be under community management of WSS services, and those where WSS services are or will be delivered by the rayon water utility. An important part of the plan should be the **affordability analysis,** confirming the financial sustainability of the recommended models.

The local population living in territories adjacent to the WSS service area should have the right to participate in the decision-making process. They can choose to be served by a rayon WSS operator, or form their own community management organisation (co-operative or association) to provide WSS services.

The rayon administration will cover initial investments to build small centralised WSS systems, and will own WSS infrastructure built in the entire rayon territory. The infrastructure will then be transferred to the Rayon Vodocanal, or will be subject to concession or lease agreements with the respective water user association or co-operative, or small-scale private operator. This will require reviewing the existing legislation related to leases and concession agreements in order to allow rayon administrations to enter into respective contracts with operators.

The Rayon Vodocanal, acting on behalf of the rayon administration, should be responsible for: a) providing back-stopping assistance to the community-based and other small-scale operators of WSS systems in the rayon (e.g. lab tests of water, leak detection, major repairs, etc.); and b) monitoring the provision of WSS services in the entire territory of the rayon.

Rayon administrations will have full responsibility for organising WSS provision on the whole territory of respective rayons. However, village administrations should help them organise community management of WSS services. Village administrations should be responsible for supporting their citizens in establishing water user associations or co-operatives, and in operating WSS infrastructure.

To deliver WSS development across a larger area, the rayon WSS Development Plans may need to be co-ordinated with, or approved by, respective oblast public authorities. Central and oblast governments should provide financial and technical assistance to rural rayons in developing and implementing WSS Development Plans (e.g. by adopting and disseminating methodological and guiding documents, providing training for officers of rayon administrations responsible for WSS, etc.).

This approach needs to be clearly established in law. The national legal framework should strengthen the responsibilities of the rayon administrations and authorise them to develop Rayon WSS Development Plans and establish Rayon Vodocanals. It is recommended that relevant legal provisions are included in the law and regulations on the WSS sector.

A legal review will be also needed for community-managed WSS services. Currently, the legal basis for community management of WSS services in Kazakhstan is the Law on Rural Co-operatives. One option is to review and adjust the existing legislation; another option is to elaborate a dedicated law specifically on water user associations and co-operatives. Given that community management of WSS services is recommended as the prevailing WSS business model in small and remote rural communities, it is recommended to adopt a dedicated individual law on water user associations and co-operatives.

It is recommended to review the existing **monitoring and evaluation (M&E) system**, and ensure its effective functioning. Existing statistical forms on WSS, for example, should include information on institutional and legal forms of WSS service delivery. Such information collected locally should be first aggregated at rayon level, and next at oblast and national levels. The information will help monitor and evaluate the institutional development of WSS services and make any necessary corrections.

The development of the WSS sector requires not only investments in infrastructure, but also in local capacity. Apart from engineering and management expertise, financial and economic expertise also needs to be developed within the WSS sector, including feasibility studies and affordability analysis. It is recommended to build the capacity of the relevant institutions, or market, with this expertise at the rayon and oblast levels.

To develop the capacity of water user associations and co-operatives, it is recommended to help them form a union or a federation at the oblast or national level. The union or federation will be a centre of needed expertise for its members and represent their interests in relation to local authorities.

The recommended WSS business models should be overseen at the national level and managed according to project management principles. Although the programme will be implemented at local level, a clearly identified implementing agency at central level[1] should be responsible for planning, legal framework development, necessary strategic and operational guidelines, and monitoring progress in developing the recommended WSS business models.

It is advised to consider a phased approach where the Rayon Vodocanals will be created and Rayon WSS Development Plans elaborated in selected pilot rayons. To facilitate scaling up the experience, all necessary guidelines and best practices (e.g. **Guidelines for Reforming Rural WSS[2],** standard contracts, a template for the Rayonal Master Plan, etc.) should be developed and pilot tested. The recommended WSS business models should be piloted in partnership with donors and international organisations that are developing WSS in Kazakhstan.

Endnotes

[1] For example, the Agency of Construction, Housing and Communal Utilities.

[2] Including a guideline on elaborating and adopting Rayon WSS Development Plan (Master Plan) and on creating Rayon Vodocanal.

Annex A.

An overview of WSS in reviewed countries

This annex presents a brief general overview of WSS in selected countries. According to the project's terms of reference, the review was initially done only for EECCA countries. However, in response to a request by the Committee of Architecture, Housing and Utilities of the Ministry of Regional Development, it was expanded to include a review of selected European countries. As a result, the review was done for the following countries:

- Armenia
- Azerbaijan
- Czech Republic
- Finland
- France
- Georgia
- Italy
- Kyrgyzstan
- Poland
- Romania
- Russian Federation
- United Kingdom
- Ukraine
- Tajikistan
- Turkmenistan

These countries represent various levels of economic development with gross domestic product (GDP) per capita based on Purchasing Power Parity (PPP) ranging from USD 2 173 (Tajikistan) to USD 36 569 (United Kingdom); population density ranging from 10 residents per km^2 (Turkmenistan) to 259 residents per km^2 (United Kingdom). Table A.1 presents the basic geographic and economic characteristics of the countries selected for the review of WSS management.

Table A.1. Basic information on countries selected for the review of WSS management

Country	Location	Land area	Population	Density	GDP PPP 2013	GDP PPP per capita 2013
		km^2	mln	persons/km^2	billion USD	USD
Italy	Western Europe	301 338	59.6	198	1 835.66	30 094.06
France	Western Europe	551 695	63.9	116	2 289.62	35 941.52
Finland	Northern Europe	338 424	5.4	16	201.74	37 012.46
United Kingdom	Northwestern Europe	243 610	63.2	259	2 391.04	37 501.70
Czech Republic	Central Europe	78 864	10.5	133	292.54	27 662.99
Poland	Central Europe	312 679	38.5	123	824.78	21 005.39
Ukraine	Eastern Europe	603 628	44.5	74	340.68	7 532.92
Romania	Southeastern Europe	238 391	20.1	84	282.35	13 251.92
Russian Federation	Northern Eurasia	17 098 242	143.7	8	2 640.74	18 670.53
Armenia	Caucasus Eurasia	29 743	3.4	114	20.83	6 128.16
Azerbaijan	Caucasus Eurasia	86 600	9.3	107	102.43	11 003.54
Georgia	Caucasus Eurasia	69 700	4.9	70	28.73	6 355.74
Kyrgyzstan	Central Asia	199 951	5.6	28	14.49	2 567.82
Tajikistan	Central Asia	143 100	8.0	56	19.30	2 373.96
Turkmenistan	Central Asia	491 210	5.1	10	53.59	9 394.35
Kazakhstan	Central Asia	2 724 900	17.7	7	248.56	14 750.46

Note: * - PPP here stands for the "purchasing power parity"

Source: various statistics.

The countries are grouped as proposed in Annex A.

Countries with a low degree of consolidation and a low degree of delegation: Kyrgyzstan, Ukraine, Poland, Finland and the Russian Federation

The water and sanitation sector in **Kyrgyzstan** can be characterised by decentralised mandates, high water losses and poor condition of infrastructure. More than 1 050 centralised domestic systems supply drinking water to the population. A majority of existing water supply systems requires capital repairs; 40% are beyond their design life and are out of order; 261 fail to comply with sanitary requirements. Some 92% of the population has access to piped drinking water. However, only 26% of the population lives in the sanitation coverage area. The process of WSS rehabilitation is constantly evolving, but a major effort is still needed to achieve a significant level of services, especially in rural areas. Community management is the prevailing business model for WSS in rural areas.

Water supply and sanitation services In **Ukraine** can be characterised by high rates of consumption of water per capita and per day, inadequate maintenance of infrastructure and insufficient financing of the WSS sector. Ukraine has relatively high water supply coverage (83.3%), but the rate of connections to the sewerage system is rather low. The main challenges for the sector are high rates of water losses and ageing WSS infrastructure. Mandates in the WSS sector are shared between the national government, regional authorities and local governments, with the latter responsible for delivering WSS services to the local population. In fact, WSS services declines with the size of the settlement. The experience of Ukraine says that a proper WSS managing model requires a balance of different administrative levels: central, regional and local, and special attention should be paid to fragmented municipalities.

The water supply and sanitation sector in **Poland** is in relatively good shape, with continuous development of the sector through national and EU funding. Polish municipalities are responsible for providing water in the required quantity and quality, as well as for sanitation services within their territory. In urban areas, both water supply and sewerage network coverage is almost 100%, while in rural areas this indicator is somewhat lower. Although the WSS sector is well developed in Poland, investment is still needed. The main focus should be on improving the situation in small towns and rural areas, especially for sanitation services. The municipal water utility is the prevailing business model for WSS in small towns and rural areas. Most are operating as limited liability companies, but there are also examples of budgetary organisations. Looking for economies of scale in the service area, some municipalities have entered into inter-municipal co-operation agreements. In this case, WSS infrastructure is extended from the city to surrounding rural municipalities, or a municipal association is established for joint operation of WSS infrastructure on larger territories. In less populated rural areas, people use individual wells and septic tanks and have to transfer sewage to a wastewater treatment plant (**WWTP**).

Water supply and sanitation services in **Finland** are well developed. Municipalities are responsible for the provision, overall development and organisation of WSS services in their jurisdiction in accordance with the Water Services Act. Municipalities may provide WSS services themselves or outsource them to private companies, but they are only responsible for the WSS sector in municipal (urban) centres. In rural areas, this is the mandate of consumer-managed **water co-operatives,** which distribute water to small villages (consisting of a number of farms and houses) or to individual households (approx. 10% of the population). Water co-operatives may be run under one of two models. In the first model, water is purchased from municipal water networks, and co-operatives take care of the investment, operation and maintenance of their own local system (distribution networks and pumping stations). In the second model, co-operatives have their own sources of water supply and are also responsible for water intake and treatment. The municipal utility of a particular region determines water and sanitation tariffs in rural co-operatives, although municipalities are not responsible for WSS services in rural areas. Municipal services in small towns and nearly all small rural co-operatives clearly run at a loss, and municipalities have to support them financially.

In the **Russian Federation**, WSS sector reforms are insufficient for the sector's needs. Despite having a quarter of the world's drinking water resources, Russia is facing considerable difficulties in solving problems associated with rational and safe water and sanitation management. In many cities and most rural areas, the existing water supply system consists of obsolete infrastructure, and investment and implementation of new technologies have not kept up with the breakdown of key assets. Municipalities organise, maintain and develop WSS services, although regional governments own WSS systems in a few cases. Only 67% of the Russian population has access to piped water services. Private operators are getting more broadly involved in the sector; however, the privatisation of the WSS sector has had some mixed results.

Countries with a high degree of consolidation and a low degree of delegation: Tajikistan, Turkmenistan and Azerbaijan

In **Tajikistan**, the State Unitary Enterprise KhMK is in charge of both WSS policy and WSS services, which are provided by subsidiary water utilities. The largest Tajik cities function outside of KhMK control; they are directly responsible for providing WSS services to their population. Community management is the prevailing business model for WSS in rural areas. At a crossroads between decentralised and centralised WSS management models, the country is considering regionalisation as another option.

On average, 57.6% of the Tajik population has access to centralised water supply services (87% of the urban population and 43% of rural residents). Although coverage rates in urban areas seem relatively high, water supply and sanitation systems are neither reliable nor safe: there are serious problems with water quality in Tajikistan. Tariffs for potable water do not cover the operational costs of WSS services, which has brought a major part of WSS facilities into a critical condition. The Tajik government has implemented several reforms, laws and national plans, and received international investments. However, a massive effort is still needed to improve the WSS sector situation. Measures should be taken to improve drinking water quality and increasing WSS coverage, especially in small towns and rural areas. Recently, with assistance from the European Bank for Reconstruction and Development (EBRD), the government of Tajikistan has been implementing a nationwide programme for rehabilitating WSS infrastructure. At the same time, it is studying whether regionalisation of water utilities could improve operational efficiency.

Most existing WSS systems in **Turkmenistan** were built between the 1950s to 1980s. As a consequence of poor management in the 20 years following the country's independence, the quality of WSS services has drastically deteriorated. Providing sufficient volume of quality water to individual consumers is still a challenge. WSS utilities have been providing WSS services on their territory since 2011. The participation of private entities in the WSS sector in Turkmenistan is marginal. About 63% of the Turkmen population is supplied with water through centralised water supply systems (84.5% of the urban population and 42.1% of the rural population). Therefore, increasing access to safe potable water has been officially recognised as a national priority.

In the **Republic of Azerbaijan**, WSS infrastructure in rural areas is not yet sufficiently developed. Water supply coverage in rural areas is estimated to be as low as 15%, and these are usually settlements benefiting from neighbouring urban WSS infrastructure. The rest of the population draws water from individual wells or irrigation canals; in some rural settlements, community-based organisations play a role in managing the provision of WSS services. Centralised sanitation systems in rural areas are very rare.

In many mid-sized and small towns, water treatment facilities are mostly dysfunctional or completely non-existent. In small towns, local water utilities operate WSS infrastructure, which are controlled by a single national operator – Azersu OJSC. It is expected that consolidated local water utilities will extend their service areas to provide WSS services to surrounding rural settlements

Countries with low degree of consolidation and high degree of delegation: France and Czech Republic

The model of WSS management in **France** is based on many small-sized municipalities (communes, each having 1 500 people, on average) that deliver WSS services. Therefore, this model is classified as one with a low degree of consolidation. However, small municipalities looking for economies of scale in WSS services may enter into inter-municipal co-operation by forming large WSS service areas. At the same time, WSS service delivery is often delegated to private companies through a contract, and from this point of view the model has a high degree of delegation. The market of private operators is strongly consolidated, meaning that a few big companies dominate the market. The business model of WSS services in small towns and rural areas is a delegation contract (which can take the form of an *affermage*, concession or management contract) with a private company. Usually it is done through a municipal association formed by several communes. The remaining communes (some 20%) use the model of direct management of WSS services, and establish their own municipal services or enterprise. Recently, there has been an ongoing discussion about private companies in the WSS sector with a visible trend towards "re-municipalisation" of WSS service delivery.

The Czech Republic uses a WSS management model similar to France. About 83% of rural residents are supplied with piped water, compared with a national coverage rate of 93.5%. According to OECD data, rural settlements (with fewer than 2 000 residents) constitute 89.8% of all municipalities; in most cases, they form inter-municipal co-operation structures to provide WSS services on larger territories.

Private operators supply most rural settlements (about 97%) with water. Under a lease contract, the operator pays a monthly fee for the municipally-owned water system in return for an exclusive right to operate it and to collect tariffs from the customers. The Ministry of Finance determines tariffs based on the value of the commodity (supplied water). This means that WSS companies do not have total freedom in setting water tariffs. The affordability of the tariff and the need to provide for reasonable profit are regulated. The WSS market is highly consolidated, with the main share of the market represented by several private companies, the largest share being held by a subsidiary of Veolia.

Countries with a high degree of consolidation and a high degree of delegation: Italy, Romania, Georgia, Armenia, and England and Wales

Water supply and sanitation services in **Italy** can be described as problematic. There is insufficient access to water due to long seasonal periods of drought and inefficient management of water resources. However, the percentage of population connected to water supply networks is rather high, at 97%. Responsibilities for WSS services are in the hands of 91 Optimal Territorial Areas (ATOs). The main issues in the WSS sector are the fragmentation of legal competencies and institutional responsibilities, along with insufficient co-ordination between all stakeholders. Other characteristics of Italian WSS services include the highest consumption rate of drinking water per person in Europe and substantial water losses due to high leakage in water networks, the average age of which exceeds 30 years. Despite several reforms in the WSS sector, further investment, especially directed at water conservation measures and renovation of the infrastructure, is required to overcome existing problems. Rural areas benefit from the regionalisation of the WSS sector; as part of ATOs, they are served by regional water utilities and pay the same water tariff as urban areas.

In **Romania,** WSS services delivery in small towns and rural areas is based on an inter-community development agency and a regional model of operations. However, in practice, it relates only to a small percentage of the rural population. Most people in rural areas rely on individual wells and tanks, as 21% of the rural population benefits from centralised drinking water supply and only 11% from centralised sanitation systems. Romania is going through a regionalisation of the WSS sector, and in the near future will make a massive effort to develop WSS in rural areas. Additional infrastructure improvement is also needed to minimise water losses and to enhance the quality of supplied water. Overall, with the help of the EU, Romania is successfully improving its WSS sector, and that trend is expected to continue.

Armenia is an example of successful implementation of regionalisation and public-private partnerships in the WSS sector. Nearly 75% of the population in both urban and rural areas are served by regional water utilities operating under a PPP model (management contract or lease contract). The remaining 25% in rural areas receive WSS services under the community management model. Recently, the government of Armenia with the assistance of KfW has been conducting a feasibility study on inclusion of the remaining rural municipalities in the service areas of regional water utilities. In the past, the local population did not accept this option because they did not want to make regular payments for water. If the option is found feasible this time, the entire country would be served by regional water utilities operating under the PPP model.

In **Georgia**, ensuring access to safe drinking water is still a major challenge. The situation in the water supply and sanitation sector is extremely complex. Most WSS systems are in critical condition due to anthropogenic contamination, non-compliance with sanitary standards and the difficult economic situation. A substantial share of water consumers experience difficulties paying for water supply services and sewage disposal. Moreover, 60% of the water pipes and half of the sewage collectors are in a dilapidated state; water quality indicators often do not meet human health and safety standards, and large quantities of water are lost to leakage in the networks (around 40% of total supply). In Tbilisi and Rustavi, the WSS systems have been privatised and are now privately owned by the Georgian Water & Power company.

WSS systems in other settlements outside Adjaria are state-owned (with the Ministry of Regional Development representing the owner), but operated by a single operating utility. Approximately half of the population has access to centralised WSS services. WSS systems are considered to be a key component in ensuring a clean environment and the good health of Georgian people, especially in rural areas.

Public water supply and sanitation services in the United Kingdom are characterised by good service quality and universal access. The WSS sector operates through a variety of institutional arrangements, which are different in England and Wales on the one hand, and Scotland and Northern Ireland on the other. In **England and Wales**, the sector is fully privatised; in Scotland and Northern Ireland, a national operator in each country provides WSS services. The percentage of the population served with supplied water and sanitation is near 100% and 97%, respectively. There is no great difference in WSS services between urban and rural areas. The high percentage of the population supplied with WSS services, as well as the shared regulatory and legislative framework, enable small towns and rural settlements to benefit from the same level of WSS services as urban areas. In England and Wales, private regional water utilities provide WSS services. Individual metering and tariff rates are uniform in the entire service area, and differences in rates depend on the zone. A national water regulator, Ofwat, regulates increases in tariff rates. A key issue concerns the condition of the infrastructure that needs to be rehabilitated to reduce water losses, not only in small towns and rural areas, but in many urban areas in the United Kingdom. Unfortunately, achieving this goal would require successive increases in water tariff rates, which may not be acceptable to the regulator.

County case studies

Case studies of the selected countries listed in Annex A are accessible at the web-link: www.oecd.org/outreach/.

[illegible]

Country case studies

[illegible]

Annex B.

Review of business models in the water supply and sanitation sector and lessons learned from their application in the EU and EECCA

Although there is no universal "one size fits all" model for the management of WSS services, and a model successfully functioning in one country may not work in another, international experience provides important lessons for developing a country's approach to WSS management. This section summarises the review of WSS management models in selected countries in Europe and Eastern European, Caucus and Central Asia (EECA). The review was part of Phase 2 of the Sustainable WSS Business Models for Small Towns and Rural Areas Project in Kazakhstan; its objective was to inform and facilitate the national policy dialogue on best possible models of institutional development of WSS in small towns and rural areas in Kazakhstan.

Since WSS is considered an essential service, WSS service delivery falls under the responsibility of public authorities. Depending on a country's public administration system, the responsibility is assigned to public authorities at a specific administrative level. In countries with decentralised public administration, the responsibility is usually assigned to municipalities, which are the lowest level of local government and the closest administrative level to the population. By assigning the legal responsibility for WSS services delivery to a specific administrative level, the legal framework designates a theoretical WSS service area. In the case of a decentralised system, it is the same as the administrative territory of a municipality. However, it is only a theoretical service area because WSS services are delivered only to the residents of the territory covered by WSS infrastructure. Those residing outside the area of the centralised WSS system have to rely on small-scale systems or individual WSS solutions. Usually the latter is the case in rural areas, while urban areas have centralised (piped) WSS systems. However, if the legal framework assigns responsibility for the delivery of WSS services to municipal authorities, they must organise WSS services in the entire territory of the municipality, regardless of whether it is urban or rural. Assigning responsibility for delivery of WSS services to small municipalities may fragment the WSS sector, creating many small and weak water utilities. Countries that face this problem have tried to reform the sector by consolidating and aggregating the WSS sector (so-called regionalisation of WSS utilities).

The review of experience in WSS management in selected countries shows two main factors that determine the choice of models for WSS service delivery:[1] the **degree of consolidation or aggregation** of the WSS sector; and the **degree of delegation** (degree of managerial and financial autonomy of the WSS operator and degree of private sector participation in WSS).

Using these two key factors, Figure B.1 classifies the WSS models of the selected countries listed in Annex A into four groups:

- countries with a low degree of consolidation and a low degree of delegation: Kyrgyzstan, Ukraine, Poland, Finland and the Russian Federation
- countries with a high degree of consolidation and low degree of delegation: Tajikistan, Turkmenistan and Azerbaijan
- countries with a low degree of consolidation and a high degree of delegation: France and the Czech Republic
- countries with a high degree of consolidation and a high degree of delegation: Georgia, Armenia, Romania, Italy, and England and Wales.

This grouping of countries is based on the contractual nature of WSS services and represents national experiences in the two key policy dimensions of consolidation and delegation of services.

Figure B.1. Degree of consolidation and delegation of WSS services in selected EU and EECCA countries

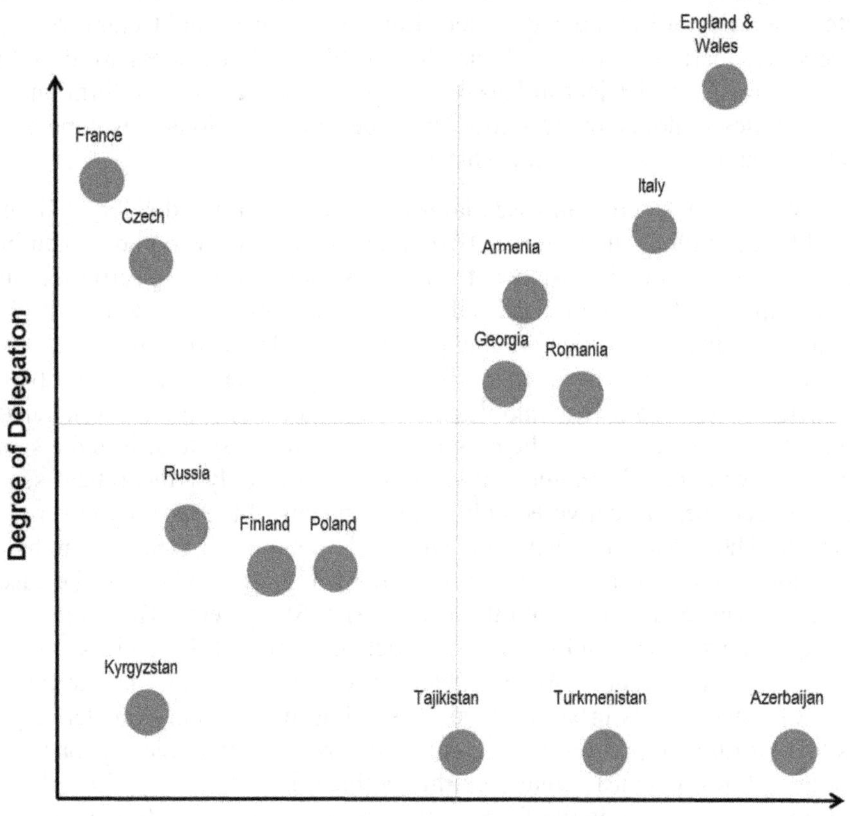

Source: Authors' own assessment.

Figure B.2 presents a classification of business models reviewed, based on the **degree of delegation** (degree of managerial and financial autonomy and degree of private sector participation) and the **degree of consolidation (aggregation)** of the WSS sector. The matrix does not cover all the possible business models of WSS service delivery, but rather shows potential models in relation to policy decisions on the consolidation of WSS services, and the autonomy of WSS service providers.

The business models reviewed are discussed below following the proposed classification.

Figure B.2. Matrix of WSS service delivery models

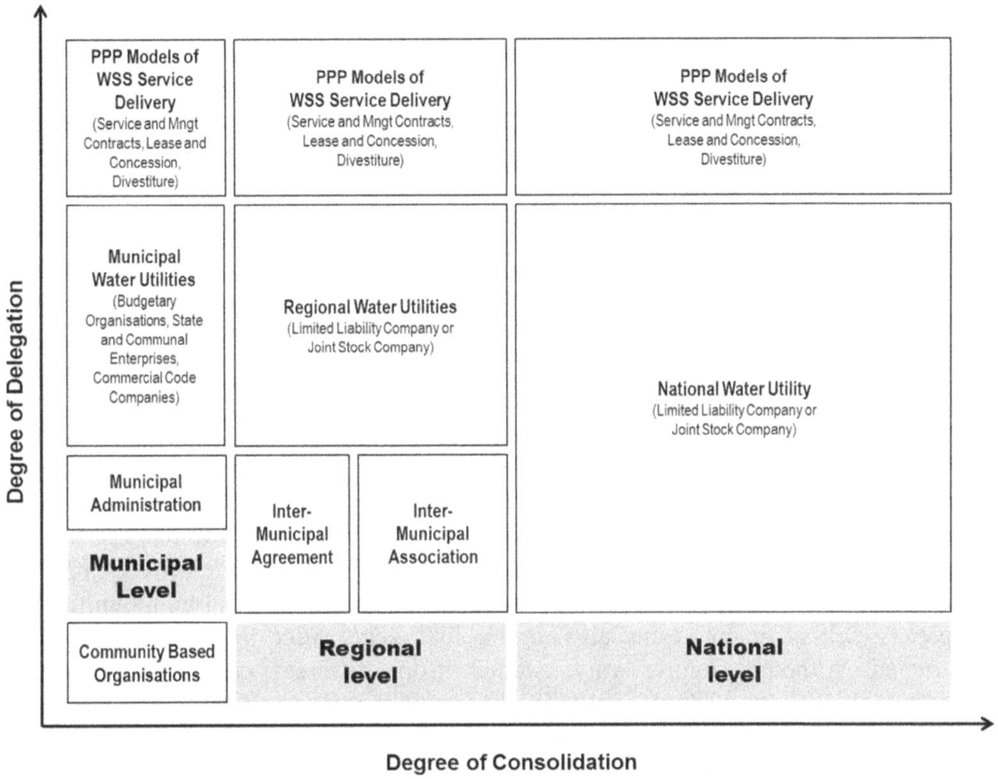

Source: Authors' own assessment.

A. WSS service delivery models classified by the level of managerial and financial autonomy

Community management model of WSS services

The community management model of WSS service delivery is a natural alternative to individual WSS systems. Usually, a small-scale WSS supplier serves a village or rural settlement, although one can find countries where this model covers larger territories. Residents of a given community form an organisation, which can have different legal forms and names depending on the country's legal framework.

This organisation, acting on behalf of residents, is responsible for delivery of WSS services. Community management of WSS services can be found all over the world, and each country develops its own specific model most suitable to local conditions. Community management has become the leading concept for implementing water supply projects in rural areas as a direct result of a broader transition from centrally planned or supply-driven approaches to demand-oriented and decentralised public governance models. The basic principle of this model is consumers' participation in decision making, community control, ownership and cost sharing. A group of residents works together to solve a problem related to WSS services and decides to build a small-scale centralised WSS system for their community. Usually with external assistance, as well as their own contributions, they make the investment and hand it over to a community-based organisation (association, co-operative) for operation and maintenance.

All residents participate in covering the costs of WSS services in the form of water tariffs or monthly fees. In addition, they contribute to the costs of rehabilitation.

A community-based organisation can operate and maintain WSS infrastructure by itself or contract out to a private company. Although there are many benefits of community-managed WSS, the model has its limitations, especially when it comes to sustaining services. It is increasingly recognised that a majority of communities cannot independently maintain their WSS systems; they require some form of external assistance over the long term.

Community management models with their many benefits have been regarded as an answer to the failure of previous supply-driven approaches for providing WSS services. These previous models often did not meet the real needs of users and resulted in systems that broke down far earlier than their designated lifespan. However, the community management model is by no means without challenges of its own. Despite the strong investment of many projects in capacity building, a significant number of systems still run into problems. Widespread evidence suggests that after a number of years of operation (or just a few years in some cases), many rural systems face a variety of problems and obstacles linked to financial, technical and environmental sustainability. It is now increasingly recognised that most communities will be unable to manage their own WSS systems without some form of external assistance. Even with improved approaches that increase local capacity, it is simply not realistic to expect rural communities to be completely self-sufficient, especially in the first years after the systems have been constructed. Although figures vary, studies from different countries indicate that approximately 30% to 40% of rural WSS systems either do not function or else operate significantly below design indicators. Constructing physical systems is an obvious requirement, but just a first step in a more complex set of actions needed to provide truly sustainable services; increased coverage does not equate to increased access to WSS services. For rural WSS systems to be sustainable, this model requires not only local capacity building measures, but also broader institutional assistance (e.g. repairs, water quality control, etc.).

Municipal management models of WSS services

Several possible WSS business models within the framework of municipal management, as well as basic models, are presented in Figure B.1. The first model is the direct delivery of WSS services by the municipal administration. This is usually applied at an early stage of WSS infrastructure development, which does not require more advanced institutional forms. In this situation, WSS services are delivered by a municipal department that employs a few technicians for operations and maintenance. This model of WSS service delivery is appropriate for small-scale WSS infrastructure with a small customer base; it would not be sufficient to ensure adequate revenue for independent service providers.

Larger WSS infrastructure requires a different approach. One alternative is to establish a budgetary organisation (budgetary unit or budgetary enterprise) for delivering

WSS services. Although strongly linked to the municipal administration, a budgetary organisation is an external entity and has more autonomy than a department of the municipal administration. The budgetary organisation model can be implemented in the form of a budgetary unit of a local public administration (LPA), or budgetary enterprise. In the case of a budgetary unit, its operations are fully financed from the municipal budget, and the revenue from water tariffs goes to the municipal budget. A budgetary enterprise is different because the revenue from water tariffs is its revenue, used for covering the costs of providing services. If the revenue does not cover the costs, the municipal budget subsidises losses. In cases of both budgetary unit and budgetary enterprise, investments are fully financed from the municipal budget. Budgetary organisations can be an option in the early stages of WSS infrastructure development, but they depend fully on the municipal budget.

An alternative model to a budgetary organisation with a higher level of managerial and financial autonomy, including investment, is the state or municipal enterprise or incorporated public company. Being fully owned by a public entity, state or municipal enterprises or incorporated public companies exercise higher managerial and financial autonomy than budgetary organisations, while remaining fully controlled by public authorities. In developed countries, state or municipal enterprises operating under a special set of laws and regulations are fully replaced by **incorporated entities** that are limited liability companies or joint stock companies. Usually, joint stock companies are used for large water utilities because the administrative costs associated with creating joint stock companies are higher than those for limited liability companies. In comparison with budgetary organisations, incorporated companies use accrual-based accounting principles and consider the depreciation of WSS infrastructure as a cost reflected in their water tariffs. They thereby generate funds for repairs and rehabilitation projects.

Because they operate under the principle of full financial cost recovery plus profit (the "cost plus" formula), the companies may also generate some funds for investment in retrofitting systems and development. Generally, the profit level of water utilities is not sufficient for larger investment programmes. For those with sufficient profits, the financial market – both local and international – is an additional option for large investments.

The model of a municipally-owned WSS operator is usually used to operate a centralised WSS system of a town or a city. It can be also used for several separate systems within a municipality, which is composed of a town and several villages. The model of municipally-owned incorporated companies can be applied only where revenue from the client base is sufficient to cover the cost of WSS services. In the case of an incorporated company, which includes the depreciation of WSS infrastructure assets in its tariffs, the price of WSS service delivery is much higher than in the case of a budgetary organisation. This means that transforming a budgetary organisation into an incorporated company will not be easy; it will require a significant increase of water tariffs and thus also additional measures to address affordability constraints.

Both budgetary organisations and incorporated companies may also provide some additional municipal services as well. This model is called **a multi-service company** (utility). It is usually implemented in small towns and villages that need all the municipal services, but have an insufficient number of residents to form a profitable client base for single service operators. In this situation, a multi-service operator is established to spread the overhead costs between all the services and thereby keep service costs affordable.

PPP models of WSS service delivery

The highest degree of delegation of WSS service delivery might be achieved in the public-private-partnership (PPP) model of WSS service delivery (see Annex C). In this case, a municipality enters into an agreement with a private company by delegating specific responsibilities for the delivery of WSS services. There are different options for PPPs, the most common of which are presented in Table B.1.

Table B.1. Public-private partnership options in the WSS sector

PPP options	Asset ownership	Operations and maintenance costs	Capital investment	Commercial risk	Duration
Service contract	Public	Public and private	Public	Public	1-2 years
Management contract	Public	Private	Public	Public	3-5 years
Lease	Public	Private	Public	Shared	8-15 years
Concession	Public	Private	Private	Private	25-30 years
BOT	Private and Public	Private	Private	Private	20-30 years
Divestiture	Private or private and public	Private	Private	Private	Indefinite (may be limited by licence)

Source: World Bank (2007).

Each model has its own advantages, inconveniences and limitations, as well as prerequisites for successful implementation. The PPP option starts with a service contract, stipulating that the private company is only involved in operating the WSS infrastructure, while the public sector incurs capital investments and commercial risks. Under a management contract or lease and concession contracts, the private sector takes greater responsibility; and finally, in the case of a divestiture, the private sector takes the greatest responsibility for the provision of WSS services.

PPP models of WSS service delivery can be applied either at the municipal or at the regional and national levels. Whatever the level, more advanced PPP models can be implemented only in cases of profitable WSS services; this is rare in rural areas with insufficient concentration of WSS customers and greater affordability restrictions. Rural areas may have examples of service and lease contracts, where small private companies operate and maintain small WSS infrastructure. Other PPP models are applied in larger territories with enough customers to ensure sustained revenue, not only for covering the costs of operation and maintenance, but also for generating profits for a private company. Usually, these models work only in large cities or populated regions.

B. WSS service delivery models by level of consolidation (aggregation)

The models of WSS service delivery presented above are relevant for municipal service areas, where the local government has legal responsibility for the provision of WSS services. As mentioned earlier, when the responsibility for WSS services is assigned to a municipality, the territory of the municipality determines a theoretical WSS service area. This is theoretical because not all residents of the municipality will automatically have access to a centralised WSS system; only residents of the area covered by centralised WSS infrastructure will have access to it. Residents outside of this area will have to rely on other solutions, usually small-scale WSS systems or individual means of self-supply.

Concurrently with urbanisation and in search of potential economies of scale, centralised WSS systems usually expand to other territories nearby, thereby offering access to more residents. The extension of centralised WSS systems can stretch beyond the administrative borders of a given municipality. This WSS service delivery model is typical of a town or a city with the status of a municipality, and where WSS infrastructure extends to surrounding rural areas that also have the status of (another) municipality. This approach, called "regionalisation of WSS services", assumes that larger service areas will provide the benefits of economies of scale and keep unit costs at the lowest possible level. As a natural monopoly, WSS services need a specific size of service area to justify economically the costs of managing a centralised WSS system. In the case of a fragmented local government system, the municipal model of WSS service delivery faces the problem of insufficient economies of scale. In such cases, the regionalisation of WSS services offers a potential solution, leading to further consolidation and aggregation of the WSS sector.

Regional models of WSS service delivery

Regionalisation in this case means providing WSS services to several settlements in more than one municipality, or assigning responsibility for WSS services to a higher regional administrative level. Regionalisation can also be defined as grouping of several service providers into a single administrative and/or physical structure. In other words, regionalisation can mean interconnection of physical systems, as well as organisational co-operation through agreements between local governments (or their utilities) to share a number of operations; this could include, for example, providing operations and maintenance services on the territory of another municipality (see Figure B.3). Regionalisation of water services can offer a range of benefits. Specifically: i) interconnected water systems can help correct imbalances in water resources among municipalities; ii) organisational co-operation can deliver economies of scale in operations (and sometimes investments) and can help improve the sector's efficiency (this is the most common driver of regionalisation reforms); iii) service providers can pool their human capacity, funds and resources; iv) differences in tariffs can be reduced due to cost-sharing possibilities (e.g. by applying a uniform tariff rate throughout the service area), thereby improving equity of access to services; and v) aggregated utilities are more likely to attract financial support from donors and, eventually, from the private sector. Access to credit and capital is also much easier and cheaper for operators with larger customer bases and revenue from user charges.

Figure B.3. Two forms of regionalisation

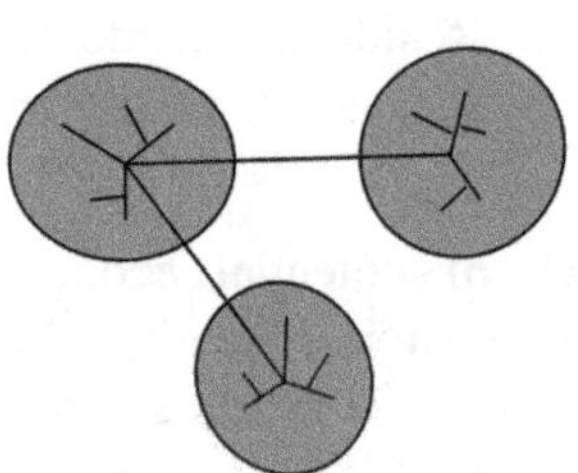

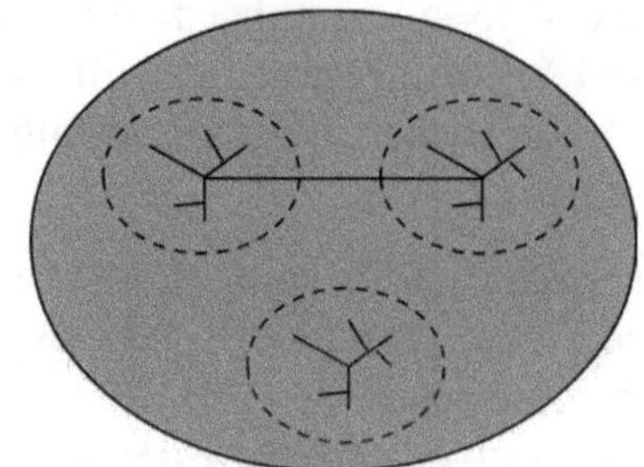

a) Physical interconnection

b) Organisational cooperation even if not fully connected

Source: Water Sector Regionalisation Review. Republic of Moldova, the World Bank, 2013.

For both forms of regionalisation, a specific legal and institutional framework for inter-municipal co-operation must be developed. Depending on the country's legal framework and public administration system, inter-municipal co-operation can have different legal and institutional forms; in general, they can take one of the following forms:

- inter-municipal agreement
- inter-municipal association
- joint commercial code company.

Under the **inter-municipal agreement** model, municipalities interested in co-operating on WSS services enter into an agreement that stipulates the purpose of co-operation and roles and responsibilities of the municipalities. For example, a municipality may decide to purchase a surplus of drinking water from a neighbouring municipality instead of building their own water treatment plant. The agreement benefits both municipalities because the former will not have to build its own water treatment plant, and the latter will generate additional revenue by using its surplus capacity. A similar agreement can be signed for directing wastewater from one municipality to a wastewater treatment plant owned by another municipality.

More integrated operations require more advanced forms of **inter-municipal co-operation**. Under the inter-municipal association model, municipalities interested in co-operation for delivery of WSS services form an association to which they transfer responsibility and authority to act on their behalf in the WSS sector. Ownership of the WSS assets by participating municipalities is transferred to the association.

Usually, the association does not actually provide the services, but establishes a WSS operator while retaining control over its operations. This situation can create problems by limiting the autonomy of the WSS operator, especially when municipalities in the association are represented by local politicians. Another weakness of this model lies in the difficulty of striking a balance between small and large municipalities in the decision-making process.

The drawbacks of inter-municipal associations do not exist in the third model of **commercial code company**. Under this model, instead of establishing an inter-municipal association, municipalities interested in co-operating on the delivery of WSS services establish an incorporated company (a limited liability company or a joint stock company). They have two options: i) to jointly establish a WSS operator; or ii) to set up a WSS assets holding company for investment planning and selecting an operator, which is typically a private company.

Each municipality then transfers its WSS infrastructure assets to the company, thus contributing to its initial capital. This initial share typically determines the deciding power of a specific municipality in company management. However, there are various solutions for striking a balance between the interests of small and large municipalities, such as the establishment of veto rules.

A different approach to the regionalisation of the WSS sector is used when responsibility for the delivery of WSS services is assigned not to municipalities, but to a higher administrative-territorial level such as a region (rayon or oblast). In this situation, regional authorities decide how to fulfil this mandate in the territory of their region, which is typically much larger than several municipalities. They usually establish a regional WSS operator, either in the form of a limited liability company or a joint stock company. The regional WSS operator delivers WSS services in the entire territory of the region and usually has branches in each town and city where there is a centralised WSS system. As with the municipal management models, different PPP models, such as service contracts, management contracts, leases and concessions, and divesture (privatisation of WSS fixed assets) could be applied at the regional level.

Any discussion of regionalisation and consolidation of WSS services must include the **concept of agglomeration**, which was introduced in the EU Urban Waste Water Directive. Article 2 of the Council Directive of 21 May 1991 concerning urban waste water treatment (91/271/EEC) defines agglomeration as an area where population and/or economic activity is sufficiently concentrated for urban wastewater to be collected and directed to an urban wastewater treatment plant or to a final discharge point. The directive does not define "sufficiently concentrated population and/or economic activity", leaving it up to individual countries. For example, in Poland, a minimum population concentration indicator is set at 120 connected people per km of sewerage network.

This idea has had a significant impact on the development of urban wastewater systems because **it defines agglomeration not based on administrative boundaries, but on the concentration of population**. It means that an agglomeration can include not only a city, but also a city (or town) and surrounding villages or several cities. It implies that several administrative entities could form one agglomeration and, vice versa, that several distinct agglomerations may cover a single administrative entity. This is a very important concept because legal responsibilities for the provision of WSS services are usually assigned according to a public administration system based on territorial-administrative divisions. The concept of agglomeration directs the attention of local policy makers to the concentration of the population and/or economic activity, and not to the administrative boundaries.

The model of national WSS operator

This model is based on the centralised approach. A national WSS operator acts more like a central government agency than a service provider. The national operator, in the form of a publicly owned joint stock company, participates in developing, and is responsible for implementing, a state policy on WSS and respective investment programme. The national WSS operator functions as an assets holding company and provides WSS services through its territorial (oblast or rayon level) subsidiaries (e.g. the case of Armvodocanal) or through the ownership of local WSS operators that provide services directly to local population, or by inviting private operators under PPP contracts.

C. Other aspects of WSS service delivery models

The above models of WSS service delivery are classified according to two key policy dimensions, namely the degree of delegation and the degree of consolidation. But these are not the only factors under consideration. To analyse the WSS delivery models deeper, one should use the following criteria:

- degree of agglomeration and regionalisation
- scope of services and the scale of operations
- degree of autonomy of the service provider
- technical and human capacity of the WSS service provision
- ownership of the WSS infrastructure
- customer services standards for WSS services
- quality and quantity of WSS services
- system for financing operations and maintenance and capital investments
- citizens' participation in decision making with regard to WSS services
- private sector participation.

D. Business models under review and their applicability for small towns and rural areas in Kazakhstan

The table B.2 below summarises WSS business models under review existing in the EU and EECCA, and assesses their applicability for the small towns and rural areas in Kazakhstan.

Table B.2. Comparison of reviewed WSS business models in the EU and EECCA

Business model	Example of countries where the business model is applied	Applicability for small towns and rural settlements in Kazakhstan
Degree of regionalisation of service provision		
Decentralised model	Austria, Moldova, Poland, Russian Federation, France	The model does not create the required economies of scale or address the lack of capacity of water/wastewater operators. The decentralised model is applicable in remote and small settlements only.
Voluntary regionalisation	Austria, Romania, Moldova, Poland, Czech Republic, France	The model addresses the problem of economy of scale and thus applies in combination with the appropriate fiscal and economic incentives. The implementation time would be long.
Obligatory regionalisation	United Kingdom, Italy, Bulgaria, Romania (with very high incentives), Armenia	The model addresses the problem of economy of scale; however, in the situation of Kazakhstan, complementary business models should be used. The implementation time will be shorter than with voluntary regionalisation.

Business model	Example of countries where the business model is applied	Applicability for small towns and rural settlements in Kazakhstan
Delegation of service provision		
Service provided directly by local governments	Austria, France, Moldova, Poland, Russian Federation, Ukraine	The model is politicised and there is a lack of corporate governance in the model.
Service provided directly by neighbouring local government (but without creating an association)	Austria, Moldova, Poland, Russian Federation, Ukraine, France	The model is politicised and there is a lack of corporate governance in the model.
Service provided directly by neighbouring local government by creating an association for water service provision	Austria, France, Poland, Russian Federation, Ukraine	The model is politicised and there is a lack of corporate governance in the model. Legislation on municipal associations is required.
Service provided directly by non-incorporated local/regional public utilities or co-operatives	Austria, France, Poland, Russian Federation, Ukraine	The model is politicised and there is a lack of corporate governance. It can be applied as a first step before the incorporation of Rayonal Vodocanals.
Service provided directly by incorporated (limited liability companies or joint stock companies) local/regional public utilities	Austria, France, Poland, Russian Federation, Ukraine	The model is applicable especially around towns (by transforming Rayonal Vodocanals into limited liability or joint stock companies).
Community based organisation/ co-operatives	Armenia, Georgia, Kyrgyzstan, Finland, Poland, Moldova,	The model is applicable especially in small remote rural settlements; it requires continuous support to CBOs/co-operatives.
Small private operators, including informal ones.	Moldova	The model is applicable, especially in small remote rural settlements.
Different levels of private sector participation		
Delegated services through the lease or concession model where public authorities retain ownership of WSS infrastructure	Czech Republic, France, Romania, Russian Federation, Italy	There is little experience on concession and leasing in WSS sector in Kazakhstan. The model would be applicable, but capacity building and amendment of legislation is required.
Management contracts	Armenia, France, Poland	There is no experience in Kazakhstan with management contracts. The sector is not attractive for private providers due to affordability constraints and tariff setting rules.
Full privatisation where private companies both own and operate the infrastructure.	United Kingdom	Currently, this model is not applicable in Kazakhstan.
Multi-service utilities	Russian Federation, Poland, Ukraine, Serbia, Italy	The model is applicable in towns where other municipal services are provided in the main town or in the entire rayon. The best approach may be to apply the model as a second step after regionalisation.

Source: Authors' own assessment.

Endnotes

[1]In this report, the terms "WSS service delivery model" and "business model" are used as synonyms.

Annex C.

Public-private partnership in water supply and sanitation sector

This annex presents an overview of the following PPP models in water supply and sanitation sector:

- service contracts
- management contracts
- leasing
- concession
- build – operate – transfer
- divestiture.

Service contracts involve "contracting out" specific operations and maintenance to the private sector, usually for several years. Under this type of contract, the public provider sets performance criteria for the activity, evaluates bidders, supervises the contractor and pays an agreed-upon fee for the services; this may be based on a fixed price for a specific term (cost-plus-fixed-fee) or on a fixed unit price basis. To achieve greater efficiency gains, contracts should be awarded through competitive tendering. Service contracts are a cost-effective way to meet special technical needs for a utility, which is already well managed and commercially viable. However, they cannot be a substitute for reform in a utility plagued by inefficient management and poor cost recovery.

Management contracts extend the responsibility of the private sector beyond individual service functions to a broader scope of operations and maintenance, usually for up to five years. If the contractor receives a set fee for services rendered, the contractual arrangement differs little from technical assistance. Under this institutional form of service delivery, a portion of the contractor's compensation is based on performance; thus, the contractor shares some of the commercial risk with the enterprise to which the service is being provided. In France, for example, where management contracts in the water supply and sanitation sector are common, incentives for productivity improvement are provided by linking the contractor's payment to indicators such as leakage reduction or number of connections. Management contracts are most likely to be useful where the main objective is to rapidly enhance a utility's technical capacity and efficiency in performing specific tasks, or to prepare for greater private involvement. Thus, management contracts can be a good first step towards more full-fledged private sector involvement if conditions make it difficult for long-term government commitment. They could also induce the private sector to undertake capital investment or accept commercial or political risk. For example, a management contract might be chosen where:

- tariffs are too low to support commercial operations, and the government needs time to increase tariffs or develop a system of public subsidies compatible with private sector participation
- the regulatory framework has deficiencies that need to be remedied before a long-term private sector arrangement can be secured
- the country lacks a good track record in public-private partnerships
- local government faces difficulties in getting key stakeholders to agree to the long-term involvement of the private sector.

In such conditions, a management contract can provide a window of opportunity for developing trust between public and private sectors, and creating a regulatory environment more conducive to private sector risk-taking.

Leasing involves a private contractor paying the public owner for the exclusive right to operate a particular service facility and bearing full commercial risk without the responsibility for major investments. A lease contract, also referred to as a franchise or licence, gives the contractor an exclusive right to the revenue stream from providing the service. This institutional form has been used for decades in water supply and sanitation systems in France and Spain and elsewhere in the municipal solid waste management sector. Under this institutional form, the public owner (lessor) remains responsible for fixed investments and debt service. In a water supply leasing arrangement, the contractor (lessee) must normally finance working capital and replacement of short-lived assets, such as small pipes. Leases are most appropriate when there is a possibility for big gains in operating efficiency, but only limited need or scope for new investment. "Pure" leases are rare, however. Most place some responsibility for investment on the private partner, if only for rehabilitation works. These contracts operate as a hybrid between a lease and a concession contract.

Concessions assign a private partner the responsibility not only for the operations and maintenance of a utility's assets, but also for investments. However, asset ownership remains with the government, and full use rights to all the assets, including those created by the private partner, revert to the local government when the contract ends, usually after 25 to 30 years. Concession arrangements exist in most infrastructure sectors, including water supply, wastewater treatment, and solid waste disposal and treatment. In a concession, investment plans and implementation are subject to review by the government authority issuing the contract. Assets created by the concession revert to the public owner upon completion of the concession. The contractor's compensation is based on the tariffs for the goods or services produced determined according to an agreement stipulated in the concession contract. The level of tariff revenue should be sufficient to cover the operational expenses, as well as debt service and depreciation on the concession's investments. Concessions are normally negotiated for periods of up to 30 years depending on the design life of the investments. The main advantage of a concession is that the private sector takes full responsibility for operations and investment, thereby creating incentives for efficiency in all of the utility's operations. Therefore, a concession is an attractive option when large investments are needed to expand the coverage or to improve the quality of services. However, administering a concession can be a complex issue for the local government because it confers a long-term monopoly on the concessionaire. The quality of regulation is highly important in determining the success of the concession, particularly the distribution of its benefits between the concessionaire (in profits) and consumers (in lower rates and improved service).

Build – operate - transfer (BOT) arrangements resemble concessions by providing services in bulk and are normally used for greenfield projects, such as a water or wastewater treatment plants. In a typical BOT arrangement, a private firm might undertake to construct a new water treatment plant, operate it for a number of years and then relinquish all rights to it to the public utility at the end of the contract. The government or distribution utility would pay the BOT partner for water from the project at a rate calculated over the life of the contract to cover its construction and operating costs and to provide a reasonable return. The contract between the BOT concessionaire and the utility usually operates on a take-or-pay basis, obligating the utility to pay for a specified quantity of water whether or not that quantity was consumed. This places all the demand risk on the utility. Alternatively, the utility might pay a capacity charge and a consumption charge, an arrangement that spreads the demand risk between the utility and the BOT concessionaire. BOTs tend to work well if the main problem a utility faces relates to water supply or wastewater treatment. If the problem is a faulty distribution system or poor collections performance, a BOT is unlikely to remedy it – and may even aggravate it. There are many possible variations on the BOT model: in build-operate-own (BOO) arrangements, assets remain indefinitely with the private partner; in design-build-operate (DBO) arrangements, the public and private sectors share responsibility for capital investments. BOTs may also be used for plants that need extensive overhauls, arrangements sometimes referred to as ROTs (rehabilitate-operate-transfer). Another variation on the BOT model is called DFBOT that is design – finance – build – operate – transfer. In this model, the private firm takes full responsibility for an investment from the very beginning, from designing it and then financing, operating, and finally, transferring the asset to the public utility.

Divestiture of water and sewerage assets (through sale of assets or shares or through a management buyout) can be partial or complete. A complete divestiture, like a concession, gives the private sector full responsibility for operations, maintenance and investment. Unlike a concession, a divestiture transfers ownership of the assets to the private sector; thus, the nature of the public-private partnership differs slightly. A concession assigns the government two primary tasks: to ensure the utility's assets, which the government continues to own, are used well and returned in good condition at the end of the concession; and, through regulation, to protect consumers from monopolistic pricing and poor service. A divestiture leaves the local government only the task of regulation, since, in theory, the private company should be concerned about maintaining its asset base. But private companies may not always take the long view. Even with an asset sale, the regulator may need to scrutinise the utility's plans for renovating or enhancing its assets. In England and Wales, the regulator requires utilities to report the serviceability of their assets.

Although widely used in other infrastructure sectors, divestitures in the water and sanitation sector have been limited to England and Wales. (Private water supply companies have also long operated in parts of the United States.) Given the national economic importance of infrastructure services, governments are generally unwilling to divest water and sanitation assets without safeguards. The UK government retains "safety net" powers to appoint another operator in case a water supply company fails. It also limits the length of the licences under which water supply companies operate.

Annex D.

Results of the Reality Check

The *Reality Check* constituted an important phase of this study. The objective was to check the feasibility of recommended WSS business models in the context of Kazakhstan, by discussing them with key local WSS stakeholders. The *Reality Check* consisted of two parts:

1. a phase of consultation at the local level with selected communities and operators representing different WSS service delivery models in Kazakhstan, conducted in June and July 2015
2. a national WSS seminar in Astana conducted on 15 October 2014.

The activities of *Reality Check* were conducted in a number of communities representing the following WSS business models:

- the Village of Chundza, Ujgurskij Rayon, Almaty Oblast – an example of the Rayon Vodocanal model
- the Village of Kokozek, Karasajskij Rayon, Almaty Oblast – an example of the water user co-operative model, named "JelSuy"
- the Village of Belbulak, Talgarskij Rayon, Almaty Oblast – an example of the PPP contract for WSS services delivery
- the Town of Talgar, Talgarskij Rayon, Almaty Oblast – an example of group water main as a source of drinking water
- the Town of Talgar, Talgarskij Rayon, Almaty Oblast – an example of small town water utility.

In all the aforementioned communities, the project team met with representatives of rayon and village authorities, management of WSS operators and the local population, including WSS services customers. At the meetings, the applicability of the recommended WSS business models and their proposed improvements, were discussed, with a focus on the Rayon Vodocanal model and the complementary model of community management of WSS services. The main outcomes of these consultations are presented below.

Ujgurskij Rayon, Almaty Oblast has a population of about 65 000 people distributed in 25 rural communities. The Rayon Vodocanal "Ujgur Su Kubyry" in ten of those rural communities provides WSS services. The rayon administration plans on extending its service area to the entire territory of the rayon.

The above examples of the Rayon Vodocanal "Ujgur Su Kubyry" and the water user co-operative "El Suy" confirm that the two recommended business models are already functioning in Kazakhstan, although they have not yet been applied in the entire country; areas for improvement still remain.

* * *

Based on very useful discussions during the first phase of the *Reality Check*, the findings and initials proposals of the study were further elaborated and draft recommendations were produced and presented at the national seminar (see below).

The national seminar on sustainable water supply and sanitation business models for small towns and rural areas in Kazakhstan was organised in co-operation with the Centre for Water Initiatives (NGO) in Kazakhstan, with the official support of the Committee of Architecture, Housing and Utilities, and Land Resources Management of the Ministry of National Economy of the Republic of Kazakhstan, and the Water Recourses Committee of the Ministry of Agriculture of the Republic of Kazakhstan. Representatives from the ministries of national economy, foreign affairs, agriculture, energy, investment and development, and Akimat of Almaty Oblast, as well as representatives of private companies, NGOs and international organisations in Kazakhstan participated in the workshop. The event helped to fine-tune the recommendations to reinforce their feasibility and ensure they would be politically acceptable for all key stakeholders in Kazakhstan: the end-users of WSS services, WSS operators and public authorities.

In the opinion of representatives of both models, a Rayon WSS Development Plan would be a very helpful management tool for WSS development at the rayon level. In addition, they agree that for the models to be financially sustainable, they should provide affordable WSS services which need to be the subject of a financial and affordability analysis at the local level. As rayon administrations should have the overall responsibility for organising the provision of WSS services, the village administration should be responsible for assisting the local population in establishing and managing water user co-operatives. The upfront investments in constructing WSS infrastructure should be borne by local authorities and the infrastructure should be subject to a concession agreement with the water user co-operative.

At the end of the national seminar, participants adopted a resolution to present recommendations of the project on "Sustainable WSS business models for small towns and rural areas in Kazakhstan" to the Committee for Construction, Housing and Utilities and Land Recourses Management of the Ministry of National Economy for their application in the formulation of WSS development policies.

Report from the national WSS seminar in Astana on 4 November 2014

The national workshop on sustainable water supply and sanitation (WSS) business models for small towns and rural areas in Kazakhstan was held on 15 October 2014 in Astana, Kazakhstan in the Zhumbaktas Hotel. The national workshop was organised under the OECD Project "Sustainable WSS business models for small towns and rural areas in Kazakhstan" with the official support of the Committee of Architecture, Housing and Utilities, Land Resources Management of the Ministry of National Economy of the Republic of Kazakhstan, and the Water Recourses Committee of the Ministry of Agriculture of the Republic of Kazakhstan; and with assistance from the "Centre for Water Initiatives".

Representatives from the ministries of national economy, foreign affairs, agriculture, energy, investment and development, and Akimat of Almaty Oblast, as well as from private companies, NGOs and international organisations in Kazakhstan participated in the workshop.

Workshop chairperson, Mr Begman Kulbayev, Deputy Director of the Committee for Construction, Housing and Utilities Land Resources, welcomed participants on behalf of the Ministry of National Economy of Kazakhstan. The current WSS business models practice in Kazakhstan and international experience in the sustainable WSS development were presented to participants. Namely, the OECD Project Team presented information on the prevailing WSS business models in small towns and rural areas in Kazakhstan, the lessons learned from international experience of EECCA and selected EU countries, as well as the conclusions and recommendations from the OECD project. Ms Ekaterina Strikileva, CAREC Project Manager, also presented CAREC's experience in developing community-managed WSS. Mr Aidos Kobetov, Project Manager, JCS "Kazakhstan Centre of Public-Private Partnership" informed participants about the development of the legal framework for PPP arrangements in WSS sector.

On the basis of the received information, workshop participants discussed possible development options and necessary actions, including:

- the question of the adoption of a law on water supply and sanitation
- the issues related to multi-service utilities
- the management of drinking water infrastructure by rural consumer co-operatives
- the issues linked to the inventory and certification of water systems in the WSS sector
- the improvement of the tariff policy for environmental impacts in the wastewater sector
- the introduction of incentives for reduction of water consumption.

As a result of discussions, participants adopted a resolution, which includes the following recommendations:

1. To pass on the recommendations of the "Sustainable WSS business models for small towns and rural areas in Kazakhstan" project to the Committee for Construction, Housing and Utilities and Land Recourses Management of the Ministry of National Economy of the Republic of Kazakhstan, for their application in the formulation of WSS development policies
2. To consider the opportunity of piloting/testing in certain areas the recommendations on the development of the rayon WSS development plan and creation of WSS rayon utilities, along with additional small-scale WSS systems, managed by local communities
3. To improve the monitoring system for WSS development, especially in the rural areas of Kazakhstan, with an emphasis on institutional development.

Project-related missions

The reports on project-related missions are accessible at the web-link: www.oecd.org/outreach/.

ORGANISATION FOR ECONOMIC CO-OPERATION AND DEVELOPMENT

The OECD is a unique forum where governments work together to address the economic, social and environmental challenges of globalisation. The OECD is also at the forefront of efforts to understand and to help governments respond to new developments and concerns, such as corporate governance, the information economy and the challenges of an ageing population. The Organisation provides a setting where governments can compare policy experiences, seek answers to common problems, identify good practice and work to co-ordinate domestic and international policies.

The OECD member countries are: Australia, Austria, Belgium, Canada, Chile, the Czech Republic, Denmark, Estonia, Finland, France, Germany, Greece, Hungary, Iceland, Ireland, Israel, Italy, Japan, Korea, Luxembourg, Mexico, the Netherlands, New Zealand, Norway, Poland, Portugal, the Slovak Republic, Slovenia, Spain, Sweden, Switzerland, Turkey, the United Kingdom and the United States. The European Union takes part in the work of the OECD.

OECD Publishing disseminates widely the results of the Organisation's statistics gathering and research on economic, social and environmental issues, as well as the conventions, guidelines and standards agreed by its members.

OECD PUBLISHING, 2, rue André-Pascal, 75775 PARIS CEDEX 16
(97 2015 37 1 P) ISBN 978-92-64-24939-4 – 2016

www.ingramcontent.com/pod-product-compliance
Lightning Source LLC
LaVergne TN
LVHW081420110826
845149LV00010B/1813